# Philosophical Essays on Free Stuff

# Philosophical Essays on Free Stuff

Robyn Ferrell

LEXINGTON BOOKS
*Lanham • Boulder • New York • London*

Chapters Throughout: *eyeline* art magazine: Some of the material was first published in Robyn Ferrell, "Glonbalisation, art market and international Market," in *Eyeline Art Magazine* no. 90, (December 2018): https://www.eyelinepublishing.com/eyeline-90/article/globalisation-art-market-and-international-art.

Chapter 6: *Hypatia* reviews on-line: Some of the material was first published in Robyn Ferrell, review: Arendt, Natality and Biopolitics, *Hypatia Reviews online*, (September 2019) https://www.hypatiareviews.org/reviews/content/420. Reprinted with permission.

Chapter 1: *Unlikely* online journal for creative arts: Some of the material was previously published in Robyn Ferrell, "Feral Philosophy" in *Unlikely*, no. 1 (August 2016) http://unlikely.net.au/docs/feral-philosophy-ferrell.pdf.

Chapter 2: *Text* journal of writing and writing courses: Some of the material was previously published in Robyn Ferrell, "Whitefella Worship" in *Text*, no. 17 (April 2013) http://www.textjournal.com.au/speciss/issue17/Ferrell.pdf.

Chapters Throughout: *Social Alternatives*: Some of the material was previously published in Robyn Ferrell, "Free World" in *Social Alternatives* 37, no. 4 (February 2019) pp5-12

Published by Lexington Books
An imprint of The Rowman & Littlefield Publishing Group, Inc.
4501 Forbes Boulevard, Suite 200, Lanham, Maryland 20706
www.rowman.com

6 Tinworth Street, London SE11 5AL, United Kingdom



British Library Cataloguing in Publication Information Available

**Library of Congress Cataloging-in-Publication Data**

Names: Ferrell, Robyn, 1960- author.
Title: Philosophical essays on free stuff / Robyn Ferrell.
Description: Lanham : Lexington Books, [2020] | Includes bibliographical references and index. | Summary: "There is free thought, free choice, the free world - and then there is free stuff. By tracking the transformations of just one idea, "free," this book describes an arc of thought through a "revaluation of values" and offers its critique in the same gesture"—Provided by publisher.
Identifiers: LCCN 2020039367 (print) | LCCN 2020039368 (ebook) | ISBN 9781793603623 (cloth) | ISBN 9781793603630 (epub)
Subjects: LCSH: Consumption (Economics)—Philosophy. | Consumption (Economics)—Moral and ethical aspects. | Liberty. | Free will and determinism. | Values. | Political science—Philosophy.
Classification: LCC HC79.C6 F47 2020 (print) | LCC HC79.C6 (ebook) | DDC 339.4/701—dc23
LC record available at https://lccn.loc.gov/2020039367
LC ebook record available at https://lccn.loc.gov/2020039368

*for Dave*

# *contents*

# *list of photographs*

# *acknowledgments*

Thank you to the following people for their help with the writing of these essays: Barbara Caine, Tina Chanter, Jason Childs, Ros Diprose, David Ferrell, Moira Gatens, Anna Gibbs, Helen Grace, Julie Hobbs, Fiona Jenkins, Jenny Lloyd, Tony Lynch, Des Manderson, Sue McGrath, Kelly Oliver, Peter Ride, Jennifer Rutherford, and Dimitris Vardoulakis.

Through the writing, I was attached at the University of Sydney in the School of Philosophical and Historical Inquiry, and at the Australian National University in the Centre for Law, Art and Humanities—I'd like to thank both for their support.

Earlier versions of some material appeared in *eyeline* art magazine, *Hypatia* reviews on-line, *Unlikely* online journal for creative arts, *Text* journal of writing and writing courses, and *Social Alternatives.*

DI
SERAFINI

# *preface*

THE SHOP WINDOW poses its query visually, at the outset.

"Why is a dress called philosophy?" the photograph asks. It takes me aback. Since when was philosophy a brand? It condenses the central problematic that begins my analysis of "free stuff."

Philosophy as a dress label becomes the point of departure for this theoretical narrative precisely because it is a figure. It is *as a figure*, which is to say as an image standing for so much more, that the place of free stuff in the contemporary cultural world can be understood.

The dress label is the first of many figures in this book of essays. Because consumer culture is driven by images, the analysis finds itself driven to them. Among the circuit of figures examined: shopping, the gift, the brand and the commodity, its global rise, the consumer's body, art and tourism, internet dating, smart phones and screenshots, divorce, real estate, and the crises in political representation represented by Brexit and Trump.

What is free? There is free thought, free choice, the free world—and then there is free stuff. The idea of free stuff encapsulates a paradox of freedom; the highest democratic value is joined with the no-cost giveaway which is something without value. This book is about the idea of free as this paradox. Priceless, and yet worth very little, almost nothing.

The spur to writing this has been the strangeness of the same word standing for something valued and its opposite. I have taken this as a clue. Freud noticed the closeness of an idea and its opposite within the desirous rhetoric of the unconscious. The reversal into its opposite is a foundation of unconscious thought. It is foreign to consciousness, and appears hostile to logic.

And yet it captures a sort of insight. In its ambivalence, the tactic renders an affinity—or, better, an anxiety—between something and its opposite. The ambivalence presents the issue as being about value.

These essays set out to fathom this ambivalence, as symptomatic of a sliding of discursive value in the time of the internet. By tracking the transformations of just one idea, "free," these essays attempt to describe an arc of thought through a "revaluation of values." And to offer its critique in the same gesture.

This book, which is both a picture book and an essay in political philosophy, offers a depiction of figures of freedom in consumer culture, a world made image by the internet and globalisation. Following an itinerary of word and image associations, it links the question of "free" to the effects of instrumentalism in the political sphere. The discussion proceeds through figures of freedom which allow the question to come into focus through diverse perspectives. Each essay is autonomous, and all are linked.

# [introduction]

# [free form]

## the toile

IN *HAUTE COUTURE*, the idea of the *toile* describes the "draft" of the garment that is produced first in calico, before risking the special fabric that it will eventually feature.

The toile allows the couturier to experiment with the form, vary the shape of pattern pieces, and to try out ideas.

The same can be imagined for the production of thought, the shapes of arguments roughed out in plain language before being dressed in philosophical garb. The method of fabrication of thought isn't much considered in philosophy. Yet it is these methods, and the forms of writing that provide *toiles* for its expression, that are now coming in for attention under pressure of the digital age. Patterns like the treatise and the monograph, published in hardback from university presses, might begin to look old-fashioned in the light of new construction methods and materials like the blog, the YouTube channel, the podcast and the tweet.

It sometimes seems discourse is no longer constrained by clear arguments and reasoned positions painstakingly developed. The proliferation of text means perhaps that no one any longer reads closely—there is just too much to read. Instead, the meme, the parading of associations, and especially the action of images mobilize conviction.

Rhetoric becomes the substance of debate. Rhetoric is foregrounded, the main event now in cultural, social, and increasingly political domains. And never more so than in challenges to liberal democratic values. These challenges take place rhetorically as scandals of representation. Fake news. Post-truth. "Trump says what I'm thinking," "Crooked Hilary," "Take Back Control," "Drain the swamp." The lies, profanity, and bullying speech of the ideologue, no less than the tendentious lures of the marketer, have become usual methods of articulation.

Jeremy Corbyn promises the British he'll pass an amended deal to leave the European Union, and then to hold a referendum on it. But Boris Johnson carries the election by simply declaring: "Get Brexit Done." Bill Shorten, Australian leader of the opposition, lays out a three-page policy arguing for healthcare reforms. His antagonist, Prime Minister Scott Morrison, answers it with brevity: "Shorten tells lies."

"Truth isn't truth!" Rudy Giuliani protests. What can he mean by this, but that deceit has entered the political discourse in such a way that to say truth is not truth is not to risk being unintelligible (even though it was a shorthand that attracted ridicule). Not only talking heads on television but people in high office making these kinds of statements to camera is evidence of a crisis in the discourse. When Kelly Anne Conway refers to "alternative facts," the important thing to take away is that when the White House says this kind of thing, it does not expect to be dismissed as making no sense. No one claims that they "misspeak"—they are speaking to a sizeable audience who hear them as speaking their language.

And maybe, in the time of the digital, thinking has changed. Critique must change with it. No longer can analysis keep out the force of rhetoric, because it is deployed everywhere to run away with the argument. It no longer works to argue facts and points of view in the face of the rhetorical extravagance of Twitter and fake news on Facebook.

At the same time, and as a response to this, it has become more pressing than ever to "speak truth to power." But the treatise is no longer working. It appears superseded. The philosophical essay is what is needed to wrest an understanding from the torrent of representations cascading around us in media streaming, and especially in the ungovernable geysers of social media outpouring. Critique must sink or swim in the multiplying public domains dominated by blandishments of the market, the promise of simulation and the movement of figures both textual and economic.

To write of the political in a way that disrupts the self-evidence of its convictions and its dogmas, and to approach a world which now contains the head-banging concepts of post-truth and fake news, requires a new way of writing. To write this not skeptically, but instead with conviction—running headlong into headlights to crash or crash through—requires me to use the form of the essay.

So, the chapters in this book attempt to show there is an associative method that leads to conclusions. There is a way that we can make sense in and of this rhetorical environment. There are ideas as strong as they ever were, concepts to be built and deployed in the time-honored habit of philosophy. Yet they need to take shape in a new way, using rhetorical strategies that move with the flows of association the better to intervene in them.

This, at least, is the attempt to essay this question of representation in the wake of digital disruption, and to show the essay as the natural form of this philosophical effort.

## high journalism

CRITIQUE MUST NOW reckon with the genre of journalism as much as with the genres of philosophy.

It must parse the shock of a good headline. "King Leer" screams a metropolitan daily, reporting allegations made in a #metoo moment against actor Geoffrey Rush during a prestigious theater production of the Shakespearian classic (the case was later to attract a significant damages award in a defamation case). "Prey to God" is the tabloid headline, on Catholic Cardinal Pell's conviction for child sexual abuse (he was later acquitted).

It must take on the power of "saying makes it so"; the claims of a "housing downturn" cause a market that lives off sentiment to slump. The superstition that naming something can possess it; the contraction "Brexit" distills a desire which inaugurates a national cliffhanger for real. While distracting from the real world pain of post-GFC austerity, it substitutes a symbolic object in the word, and "Brexit means Brexit."

Journalism leads with the punch/line, news coming right to the point with no preamble. It seizes on the packaged thinking of the glib phrase (the trope fits on a t-shirt). The neologisms of journalism concentrate the stain or the portent in the indelible phrase or figure—the IC or "involuntary celibate," the "lame duck" president, the "rom cons," the fat chick, slut-shaming, gaslighting and so on. It adopts the potency of patois and street talk to "tell it like it is" and more, to point up your worst fears of it.

This presages a new way of thinking as much as talking. The pyramid structure of the standard news report means the topic is relayed from the top down. Beginning with the most current happening, subsequent paragraphs add salient detail working backward from the event. Only then will the article expand into background or context—but you don't have to read that far to grasp the news. There is no conclusion. And the subeditor cuts from the bottom to fit limited (commercially valuable) space.

This journalism is open all ears but has limited attention; the event is interpreted according to a syncretic, even iconoclastic, analysis. An active poetics arises from this, populated by the figure, figures, and the figurative. This poetics grows out of the postmodern, reflecting on the features of no fixed points, no guaranteed reference, no unquestionable authority, no hierarchy of knowledge, no canon. It is no longer taking dictation, so the risks are great—of meaninglessness, of nihilism, of slander and of banality. Making meaning becomes a critical activity in many senses; of critique, but also timely to the point of being urgent and borne of crisis.

To make an active poetics out of essayism requires pushing back against what Adorno and Horkheimer analyzed as the "culture industry," an economic-cultural hybrid that commodifies every form of expression, at its worst colonizing experience and negating thought. It is not well-meaning. The culture industry insinuates itself into representations either by infecting its language and style, or in the underlying territorializing of the space of representation. But its priorities are outside representation; they are not aesthetic, they are in all cases commercial.

Take as an example the opening up of the radio spectrum to commercial proprietors in America in the 1930s. Paul K. Jones writes of how this spawned a host of ideologues populating a space that was conducive to advertising. A contemporary parallel exists in television licensing that allows Fox News to set a political agenda parading Trump and his acolytes for an audience to deliver profit to Murdoch media interests and those of its advertisers.

However, television is yesterday's news when compared to the internet, which is the culture industry on steroids. What began as a dream of a communication commons, in which all might express themselves freely and for free, is now carved up into multinational fiefdoms reaping huge profits from digital enclosures. How can critique even compete, in a cultural space so dominated by commercial priorities?

## Nietzsche's pedigree

THE POSSIBILITIES OF this essayism grow out of critical theory, out of its cousin "post-structuralism," and out of what is generally known in Anglophone terms as "European philosophy."

But the virtue of writing aphoristically has long been harbored in philosophy. This essayism is something old and new. From Heraclitis to Nietzsche, philosophy has often sought this brevity of thought and its action of allusion.

The essay attempts. *Essayer* in French: "to try" (Montaigne is credited with the first essayism.) The essay tries out ideas and writes strategically. In "The Essay as Form," Adorno describes it as a philosophical form. Because subjects today need the reticence of hypothesis, and because of an ambivalence about authority and tradition, critique calls for the essay over other forms, as a philosophical gesture.

The essay need not be this, has not always been so, but to write philosophy now might necessitate a kind of essayism. Adorno's assertion of essayism and style as the essential prophylactic in writing philosophy is more timely than it was when he wrote it (in 1954–58). In all senses, as criticism, as disgruntled judgment and as pro-active prescription in a crisis of concepts, critique now needs the philosophical essay.

The essay Adorno describes is a refined practice using all the resources of philosophy and rhetoric to achieve its version of weightlessness. Although presented as observation, Adorno's idea of essayism is normative; he describes a philosophical procedure which also dictates a philosophical complex. There is no nature nor second nature here; the essay balances atop a pyramid of concretized moments and crystallized dialectics, owning none of them except as footholds. The essay is an aerialist.

And in its play, the essay is deadly serious about philosophical thinking after philosophy; the "newness of the new" trumps the novel as the elastic form for modernity (and more so, for post-modernity). Profoundly ironic, Adorno has already guaranteed at the opening of his essay that what doesn't meet this esoteric self-imbrication risks falling to earth as a "bad essay," merely rehearsing the forms of philosophical-scientific-logical received wisdom. It begs the question: How does a form of writing function in its intellectual time and place to engender intelligibility, to provoke legibility? This is the philosophical-rhetorical question to which Adorno draws us.

Nieztsche addressed this in the aphoristic styles of the *Gay Science*, the narrative fragments of *Thus Spake Zarathustra*, the bellicose portraits of human nature in the *Genealogy of Morals*. Gillian Rose is right to say that Adorno's essay is a paean to Nietzsche, although it is a loyalty honored more in the breach. Unlike Nietzsche, Adorno does his essayism as heavy-handed emphatic dogmatic-seeming hyperbole at odds with the airiness he eulogizes.

While Adorno is its consummate theorist, it is Walter Benjamin who is the practitioner of the essay and Nietzsche's stylistic heir.

The essay's "innermost formal law is heresy," Adorno writes. "Through violations of the orthodoxy of thought, something in the object becomes visible, which it is orthodoxy's secret and objective aim to keep invisible." The essay is the move that might, in Deleuze's words in *Difference and Repetition*, "take philosophy from representation to abstraction."

Making meaning sideways in the peripheral vision, through affect, homophony, juxtaposition, spacing—these figures were named in medieval poetics in the recondite terms of synecdoche, catachresis, metonymy, metaphor. It was Ricoeur who revitalized them in *The Rule of Metaphor*. The essay adopts a Freudian method, outlined in *The Interpretation of Dreams*. Nothing less than a rhetoric is described by Freud there, where familiar figures from the historical discourse are subsumed under two complementary principles—that of condensation and displacement.

As Lacan later refines it, this amounts to associations made according either to similarity/difference or propinquity/spacing. New rhetorical principles emerge—of sequence, threading, image, association, contrast, repetition—in the rhetorical means of the essay. Now philosophy is not just offering commentary, nor taxonomy on rhetoric—these figures become its stuff. New proponents emerge: Deleuze, Lyotard, Derrida, Zizek, Irigaray.

The aphoristic offers formal possibilities, then, that are both old and new to philosophy. For the purposes of a revaluation of values, the aphorism would allow for a free form of writing, to open out a horizon without closing in on it, to make proposals seem more stark or more tentative, to give space to an idea to assume a novel shape.

Writes Wittgenstein of going to his tailor: "What does a person who knows a good suit say when trying on a suit at the tailor's? 'That's the right length,' 'That's too short,' 'That's too narrow.' Words of approval play no role, although he will look pleased when the coat suits him" (1966, 5).

An aphorism is philosophy with pins in its mouth, taking in a seam, letting out a tuck, deploying the requisite skill for the textual material. Aphorism is a way of making philosophy, and it is an aesthetic means, a method both for judgment and expression.

## spacing

AN IMAGE IS as it depicts, and a figure is an image that stands for something else. Spacing is more subtle; something you don't see. The sequence in which things appear, the forms that wrap them in coherence come prearranged as genres, which is to say as expectations and even formulae for rhetorical shape.

What is philosophical about the essay form? Here are some of the theorists whose intuitions underpin the following essays, and whose texts are discussed there in more detail:

It is Bakhtin who observes the taking shape of intelligibility in the clothing of the "speech genre." Granting that all language use (not only literary forms), to be intelligible must conform to previously developed rules of composition, Bakhtin approaches their heterogeneity in his essay, "The Problem of Speech Genres."

Baudrillard, with the concepts of "simulacrum" and the "hyperreal," knew more than he declared about how this mode of expression would play out. In his analysis of the Nixon White House (in *Simulacra and Simulation*) his profound Marxist suspicion of the play of Capital in the space of political representation ignited, capturing the tropes of the developing digital consciousness.

But perhaps the single most important analytical intervention in the understanding of the digital rhetoric is Derrida's concept of *différance*. As the observation of an ineluctable spacing that lubricates the flow of articulation, he could describe the mechanics in any text and how it allowed meaning to slide.

Foucault's grasp of what will be called "emergence," in which material situations are seen to grow up, proliferate and assume new qualities around designated structures, also matters. Language becomes discourse, the body becomes biopower, space becomes furnished as the prison, the school, the asylum and the court.

Arendt's magisterial study of totalitarianism enacts the genre of a philosophical history as it shows the political danger of the present way of thinking it. Especially in the third part of *Origins of Totalitarianism*, Arendt uses historical features to delineate a kind of thought characteristic of the political.

And the dark figure of enlightenment and its underbelly, instrumentalism, is captured by Adorno and Horkheimer's powerful amalgam of psychoanalysis and Marxism in the figure of the culture industry, as outlined in *Dialectic of Enlightenment* and subsequent writings.

Three slogans provide the philosophical backstory to free stuff—summary responses to the cultural revolution of the internet and the digital:

*Technology is a way of thinking*

Martin Heidegger wrote about technology before much of what we live with today came to pass. He is still prescient; before there is technology there is a way of thinking. Technology is a way of thinking, a way of imagining the world as being there for the taking, defined by an instrumentalism. Although specific technologies could end tomorrow, the mindset that gives us technology—imagining the world as a resource and a reserve for our use—could persist. He raises it as an ethical question, whether we can afford our whole lives to be colonized by the instrumental in this way.

*In the future, everyone will be famous for fifteen minutes*

Andy Warhol, the pop artist whose large canvasses brought to book the fine art feint as distinct from commercial art, saw what mass information systems could do before the internet came online. In the 1960s and 1970s, in "the Factory," he experimented with popular culture and declared: "In future everyone will be famous for fifteen minutes."

This democratizing of fame and celebrity suggests everyone gets their moment in the sun. The flipside is that sustaining notoriety, and even concentration, will be difficult. The internet deals in currency, in things that are here and now. Yesterday's celebrity is already a genre; "where are they now?" The former stratification of culture, where the rich and famous, the great and the good were admired from afar, has been greatly modified by the DIY of social media and the dream of "going viral," even if only with a cat photo.

*The Gulf War did not take place*

And there is the more somber analysis of Jean Baudrillard's summation that "The Gulf War Did Not Take Place." This was not a war but a spectacle devised for mass broadcast; what was seen of this conflict was TV footage from CNN, a simulacrum of war made for television. No fighters, no territory, nor casualties on the ground for the US.

The possibility of images taking the place of realities is now propelled by the internet. This is difficult territory for culture to find itself within. Behind enemy lines, in a hard place—not finding its material grounding, but imagined in myriad ways by manipulating images. This simulation begs the question of what we want from our cultural lives, let alone how we might understand ourselves.

The chapters that follow explore these paradoxes of freedom in the internet age. They do so using this essayist method, making philosophy akin to high journalism, which becomes the best chance of tracking concepts across the field of the digital.

*market values*

## *[one]*

# *[free gift]*

I'M HANDED A free sample as I'm shopping. It's for a face cream called the "ultimate miracle worker."

It starts me thinking about "free." There is no such thing as a free gift. Free stuff is an enticement offered to consumers to get us engaged. It works because not everything is free. Zero is a unique number that behaves unlike other numbers. Offering a product for free puts it in a different category from any other price at all. Make it one cent and you change the ploy—and ruin its effectiveness—by precipitating us back into a scale of monetary value. As purchasers, we automatically begin the calculus about whether the stuff at that price is "worth it."

In *Free*: *The Future of a Radical Price*, Chris Anderson wrote about how the "zero price gambit" could be profitable by luring consumers into the zone of a transaction. Not quite a "bait and switch," the zero price strategy still ends up working by promising one thing and delivering another. The gift is an old strategy that anthropologists have identified across societies for cementing good will and obligation.

This free gift poses our query visually from the get-go: "why?" The sample of face cream handed out at the cosmetics counter of a department store starts a chain of associations. We know the sample is a marketing gambit that is actually a claim on the shopper's attention. The free gift distills the paradox. Freedom is at the same time the highest democratic value, anchor of the political philosophy of modernity, and the word for a giveaway of almost no value, inconsequential and something had "for free."

That the gift takes place in a department store is significant because it is within consumer culture that we find the "why?" of this paradox. It takes place as a creature of a free market and in the logic of exchange. It takes its place in the free association of images of the real world in the internet age.

## phenomenology of shopping

THE PHOTOGRAPH IN this chapter is of Bon Marché, one of the first department stores to be opened in Paris—in 1852 on the chic left bank. The department store is the first space to operate according to consumer logic, where the wares are on display on shelves and not closed up behind the counter, mediated by the seller.

The goods are out there where you can see them, close enough to touch. Things incite you to touch them, to begin a relationship with them, imagine them being your own. This is essential to consumer logic: that you should think yourself together with this object, however briefly, however unconsciously. Do I want this? Is this what I need? Is this me?

The new plan for a shop, as embodied in Bon Marché, changed the character of the shopping transaction completely. Shopping became an intransitive verb—to shop. We went from buying things because of their functional value to shopping for things for their psychological action on us—to appropriate to the shopper the luster and prestige of the thing offered for sale. The seller drops from view; the transaction is now an emotional one between myself and the stuff.

Department stores made spaces that created a milieu for this new way of buying things. They were conceived as luxurious, aspiring spaces of beauty and even of some magnificence, in the style of the palaces of the rich—only these were spaces everyone could visit and dwell in, enjoying the ambience for the time of the shopping trip. Selfridges, Macy's, and Galeries Lafayette all feature the department store formula of mood lighting, elegant fixtures, and decorated spaces. Look at how, in the picture, the whole of the cosmetic floor glows with the glamour of lights and ornament. The design of the escalators as seen from the gallery level draws us up into this Aladdin's cave.

The experience of being in this space can be at once undemanding—drawn up without effort by a moving staircase, overlooking vistas of possibility—and exciting. Will I find what I'm looking for? The pleasure only makes sense as an emotional exploration. Shopping is a kind of pleasurable anxiety, a persistent impulse toward something I don't yet possess, stimulating a sensation that I am incomplete. "Retail therapy" is hardly a joke; it is an adventure of the ego.

This explains the emotional payoff in it; otherwise shopping would just seem exhausting and repetitive. Indeed, some people find it so—the legendary executive who leaves it to his wife to do the shopping except for an exasperated run around on Christmas Eve, which, if he's lucky, he may even delegate to his PA.

This man is stereotypically a boss; if production is the masculine pursuit, then shopping is a feminine one, a quest initiated by the gender that makes attachments readily, who is sociable, caring, and insecure. Shopping is women's work.

The consumer and the producer present two parts of a *pas-de-deux*; while the producer is perhaps more lauded in the images of economic value, and the consumer can be seen as someone with the easier part to play in the economy, nevertheless consumption is economically mandated by commodity production. So economic journalists can talk of a "consumer-led recovery" without irony.

Coming down the escalators in Selfridges, billboards appear at eye level and then disappear over my head. "Buy me, I'll change your life" they say, tongue-in-cheek, as they come to meet me. The milieu of the Department Store is also the incubator of the dark art of marketing, an art of persuasion. Begun as the sly blandishment of small desires ("we both know you are not rich, but you can feel rich for an afternoon in this space"), marketing is now the science of manipulation. It is now a whole body of knowledge devised out of the disreputable twins of psychology and rhetoric, with some neuroscience and statistics thrown in.

More billboard philosophy: "I shop therefore I am." The flippant reference captures the surprising logic of consumerism, gullible and cynical at once. Consumerism, in its aspect as desiring consummations, runs the risk of being gullible. Witness the willing submission of consumers globally to The Brand™: McDonalds, Prada, Nike, and so on. Food, clothing, and footwear are all strangely emblematic of our social investments as embodied in stuff. It seems we desire capitalism, or anyway we crave its satisfactions. We want stuff.

Of course the department store is being crowded out now by shopping online. Nothing is perhaps more dispiriting than the overwhelming preoccupation of the web with this consumer pornography. This manufactured phantasmagoria is essentially about investment and projection—and only sometimes about the explicit furtive kind that goes on in the dark (web).

## the brand

CONSUMER THINKING—the strange lure of stuff—is embodied in the brand.

It's no accident that the brand has grown up most visibly around clothes and apparel, because the projection of value onto stuff, necessary for consumer logic, works most naturally out of our embodied self-regard.

Our body is what other people know of us; because of this, it is the foundation of our social image and value, and nothing is perhaps more sincerely felt than the desire to look good. To look prosperous, stylish, to "look the part" or at the very least to look normal. The fashion faux-pas is a very particular kind of pain for the wearer, and something that can send anyone scurrying home to change.

After all, a primary function of dress, as Anne Hollander observes in her benchmark study *Seeing Through Clothes*, is to make the wearer look real. Looking real is looking like you "grew there," like you belong to that milieu and are not odd, miscreant or mad. Looking real demonstrates that you know how to fit in.

The move to the brand took root early in haute couture. For example, the clothes of Dior and Yves St Laurent now feature in galleries in the Victoria and Albert Museum and the Berlin Kraftwerksmuseum. They went from desirable artisan product to work of artistic genius in several quick steps.

"People made clothes for years before any became a tailor," Marx remarks in *Capital*. It was an English tailor, Charles Frederick Worth, who became the first "fashion designer." He set up the first haute couture house in Paris in 1858 to sell luxury fashion to wealthy women. *Le Chambre Syndicale de la Haute Couture* was established in 1868 to protect and define the new entity of designer fashion.

The gradual evolving of the labor of tailoring into the fashion commodity was accelerated by moves to mass production. By the end of the nineteenth century, some designer fashion had migrated into the department stores and in the twentieth it moved onto the High Street as *pret-à-porter*, ready-to-wear, fashion. Designer labels began to sell "the look" to a mass market.

Ready-to-wear led to a standardizing of the consumer body, imposing the pre-existing schema of sizes onto the individual wearer that was inherent in mass production. Gone was the notion of individual tailoring, except for the very wealthy, but gone also was the idea of clothes made to fit a particular body—an idea that had been available to all wearers, however humble, in times past. Ready-to-wear was a far cry from making your own clothes from ordinary material; as mass consumerism grew it became less and less of a boast to claim "I made it myself." The home dressmaker has quickly found herself wearing things that make her look beyond the pale, cast out of Hollander's zone of "looking real."

The home-made dress had the virtue of being constructed around a body that was as it was. Its measurements were individual, and the idea of it falling short of a standard made little sense. It has been replaced by an idealized version of that body, the mass produced body. Individual bodies now need to live up to the aspiration of the size ten, or worse, the size two. In turning one's body into the consumer platform, ready-to-wear clothing teaches us anxiety about our actuality.

Ready-to-wear had other consequences for the social body. The most obvious was the providing of the means for everyone to participate in an idea of self-image and self-promotion through the idea of "the latest fashion." It produced a paradox in the notions of price-points and luxury items that continued to sustain the age-old role of clothes to distinguish their wearers' social station.

## the body as stuff

HAVING BEEN CONSCRIPTED into consumerism through the essential social practices of dressing and eating, consumers are solicited even in their free time to watch the compelling horror show of consumer logic on reality TV.

In a previously popular reality TV show, "The Biggest Loser," the production of the normal body as a function of fashion, diet, and other consumer pursuits is reinforced by its counter-image, the grotesque unreality of the fat body. The "proper bodies" of the coaches are pictured as exemplar, while the obese bodies of the contestants enact the anguished drama of failing to conform.

The idealizations of the feminine body in particular progressed in tandem with the over-bountiful Western diet across the twentieth century to incite the practices of exercise and weight management. As a form of social engineering, these practices came to decree what was the normal height and girth of the human person.

A study in the 1940s aimed to establish through measurement the standard body type of the American, and was assisted by a newspaper campaign that sought to find "Norma," the statistically normal woman (the search is chronicled by Elizabeth Stephens). Her statue, along with her mate, Norman, was erected in the Cleveland Health Museum in 1945 and readers of the local newspaper were invited to submit their "vital statistics" to a competition whose prize was the owner of the statistics being crowned as the real life Norma. Ironically, being a mathematical average, Norma was hard to find. But this didn't arrest the search for norms of self-improvement throughout consumer culture from the mid-twentieth century on.

This schematizing using the generalizing properties of statistics became an aspect of the wider social techniques in public hygiene policy directed at organizing populations. It went further, and prepared the torment of the eating disorder from anorexia to obesity.

It all goes to show the phenomenology of consumerism—the lived experience of being a consumer—is about what we must become in order to engage the world according to norms. Norms are everything—they are the way we are socially bonded. "All people are equal" equals "all are equivalent" ergo "all are the same." We are taught to strive to be like others and to see that differences (if they can't be ironed out) don't matter.

To the extent we are different we differ only as brands do, as different versions of the same stuff. To really differ is to stick out and not in a good way. While brands strive for their "point of difference," ironically, this is against the background of same-same.

At the same time, an undertow of prejudice is pulling down those whose difference is deemed to matter: race, sex, sexuality, disability—all states of the body that create difference for myself and my others. A totalitarian scheme of social purity and bodily perfection shines out of "The Biggest Loser" with a scary black sheen. This show is global, but we are all embodied. We become ourselves the commodities.

## consumer logic

HOW DOES THE brand work to suspend argument and conscious appraisal, engendering this regression to "I want?"

The commodity is powered by an image logic that gets around other methods of evaluation. Because shopping is a way of being in the world, a way of relating to it, it leads us to thinking, and to the way of thinking that belongs to the commodity. The phenomenology of shopping leads us to consumer logic.

The commodity is not just the thing itself but something that happens to stuff that prepares it for consumption. And this "something" is not merely the addition of processing, arrangement or presentation. Commodifying things means adding an idea to them; it is indeed a way of thinking about the material world. Commodifying means adding an overlay of value to something that can only be found in exchanging it.

The commodity is found in the difference between the use-value of something and its exchange-value. From when someone makes something for someone else's use, we have a commodity. It also marks the beginnings of the division of labor in a community, and the point at which investments get going.

The commodity is above all a unit of exchange, and its circuitry runs on desirability—a commodity is something someone wants. The commodity, whether it's a widget or a water bottle or a work of art, packages desire in a way that can be consumed. It completes the relationship between myself and my objects, conditioned through my needs and wants, as a style of consumption. And in the consumption we have its "production of value." The commodity is sold; whoever owns it is enriched, and whoever buys it is satisfied. In theory.

There is an uncanny materialism in the commodity, founded on investments and projects and indebted to fantasies that are animated in our social relations. It's called commodity fetishism, making things haunted by value. In the idea of commodity fetishism, adding exchange-value to use-value turns out to be adding nothing more than value.

How things become commodities is illustrated in Marx's lucid example of the table, presented in Volume One of *Capital*: It begins as wood shaped by someone's labor, and fashioned into a table, solid on its legs. This gives it a use-value. But once it becomes something for sale it acquires an exchange-value, and from there Marx imagines it as something more uncanny. He imagines it "stepping forth" as a commodity. "It is changed into something transcendent. It not only stands with its feet on the ground, but, in relation to all other commodities, it stands on its head, and evolves out of its wooden brain grotesque ideas, far more wonderful than 'table-turning' ever was."

These "grotesque ideas" include the value of its provenance (Ikea versus genuine Chippendale), the story of its production (designed by Bauhaus architects or made up from a flatpack) and all the added qualities of brand and status markers (seen in *Vogue*, discarded in a garage sale) that are layered on it like several coats of paint.

The brand is an elaboration of the idea of the commodity. The brand is a commodity that has been completely abstracted from its material. It floats now above the stuff it is made out of, making the handbag or the trainers into a "product." It's as though the use-value had been swallowed up by the exchange-value so that the price bears no relation any longer to the thing's production, who makes it and from what. By far the greater part of the price of a Chanel garment or a Hermès bag is paying for the brand. Even though there is the pitch that it incorporates the best design and best quality materials, in fact we know that today these objects are made in factories across Asia that are neither luxury nor artisan studios.

Commodity fetishism describes the more-than-material that propels value creation. The making social of things and the making thing-ly of the social bond is critical to understanding value creation in the era of the internet. This creation of value relies on projection; on the one hand, the anthropomorphizing of things in a kind of making-religious. And on the other, making social relations thing-like and real. The creation of the desired relation as an object embodied in the commodity is fetishistic at least in the anthropological sense if not in the psychoanalytic, of worshipping something invested with sacred significance. By this reasoning, free stuff and its attendant rabid consumer culture is an embodied projection of this fetishistic sort.

It is what I am invested in that propels me into consuming. Ironically, free stuff is very unfree, although it may appear "cost-free," since it engages complex potent figures from inner fantasy and binds these to present choices. So the word fetish becomes the focus, as much as the word commodity, in commodity fetishism. In the shadow of the passivity of consumer culture lies a threat that this mode of value could empty out our cultural accounts and destroy our symbolic investments, leaving only the branding.

The international nature of this consumer logic is demonstrated in the spectacle of CapitaLand's Raffles City shopping mall in Shanghai. Five glamorous stories of glass and chrome revolve around an atrium bedecked with a spiral staircase. It expresses the action of global capital for which national borders are no object. CapitaLand, a Singapore-based real estate trust, boasts more than $100 billion in assets across the world.

Global commerce soars high above the sovereign states and their systems of border policing, excise collection and regulatory labor law. From its position in this ether, cynicism comes to haunt the multinationals behind the brands, chasing "shareholder value" above ethical and sovereign constraints.

Free trade allows what is produced to be made at the lowest price possible globally, but sold at the First World premium—product imported, profit exported, tax avoided. The power of the multinationals is now greater than individual governments who anyway are beholden to them for whatever contribution they care to make to employment, investment and social funding.

Of course the large conglomerates that own the many consumer brands of clothes and luxury goods are not united, but in competition. Yet increasingly brands are scooped up into cartels—for example, the conglomerate LVMH owns luxury brands across the range of commodities including champagne labels Moet & Chandon, Dom Perignon, Krug, Mercier and Veuve Clicqot; Hennessy cognac and Domaine Chandon wines; fashion brands Céline, Dior, Emilio Pucci, Fendi, Givenchy, Kenzo, Marc Jacobs, Loewe, Louis Vuitton, and R. M. Williams; perfume and cosmetics brands of these fashion houses and others including Guerlain, Benefit and NUDE; jewelers and watchmakers Bulgari, De Beers, TAG Heuer; and the department stores le Bon Marché and DFS. This list is not exhaustive.

Even intellectual and cultural products are now subject to this global aggregation. Lexington Books—which this book is published under—is an imprint of academic publisher Rowman & Littlefield Publishing Group, which includes more than forty other imprints at last count.

## the status of the gift

TO PAY THE market price for something is to get a fair exchange; to agree to an equivalence between the goods and the money. Even a barter exchange is an agreement of equivalence between two things of different kinds.

But the gift is of another order. If the gift is powerful, it is because its nonreciprocal character opens up a different way of valuing things. It leaves the giver empty-handed and so is not a transaction of equivalence. We know this from the exchange of gifts with relatives—while I may feel I never get as nice a present from certain relatives as the ones I give to them, such resentments can only be shared behind the hand. A gift does not entail equivalence, in the way that a purchase does.

The giveaway is a psychologically complex gesture that engages registers of meaning and obligation beyond the straightforward economic transaction. It is like this because the resonances around the word "free" are so much more than just monetary.

This isn't to deny that the gift entails something. In *The Gift*, anthropologist Marcel Mass contrasted two orders of giving and receiving in his study of societies. In modern western society, the system of monetary exchange is highly developed and provides the main channel of exchange between members. But in more traditional societies the giving of food and hospitality is designed not as a straightforward swap, but as a gesture to increase the honor and prestige of the donor.

"The unreciprocated gift makes the person who has accepted it inferior," writes Mauss, and "charity is wounding for him who has to accept it." Tribespeople from different clans may give more, and more extravagantly, to other clans so as not to be outdone.

These two economies apply between social groups and particularly between groups of men, which is Mauss' focus. But there is another kind of giving—the giving of care for example—that can be identified more with the domestic and the feminine. This giving may exceed exchange in a different way, as a kind of pure gift that is nonreciprocal. Because of this, it can become equivocal—think of the mother who gives everything for her children and is despised by them on that account; or someone who lavishes care on a spouse or relation only to have that contribution belittled or taken for granted.

The character of the gift can be more powerful than purchasing; we say "I cannot thank you enough" when someone does us a favor. "How can I ever repay you?" we ask, especially when the gift is great. To give the gift of life, in the saving of life or in hazarding your own safety to give aid, is to give of yourself with an unmatched generosity. On this is built the veneration and gratitude expressed to the war dead, and for others who give their lives in the course of duty. This kind of giving, the giving without return, goes closer to a notion of sacrifice.

## democratic freedom

"THE PRICE OF freedom is eternal vigilance;" this catch-cry, commonly attributed to Thomas Jefferson but probably from an earlier Enlightenment orator, is to be found on commemorative statues, low-rise facades and above the bars of returned servicemen's clubs.

It commemorates another kind of freedom; political freedom. The price of this freedom is not zero. For some of the enlisted, the cost was the highest that can be paid—their lives given in their youth. "Age shall not weary them nor the years condemn," as the verse runs, quoted in those clubs on ceremonial days.

Freedom is arguably the highest value of a democracy. It is enshrined in constitutions and bills of rights throughout the "free world." It is the precondition of democracy because political choice can only be meaningful in a system where citizens are free to exercise it. So free thought, freedom of movement, freedom of association and free speech are part of a cache of freedoms that underwrite this "government by the people for the people."

The armed forces secure the defense of the country's constitution in a time-honored pact of citizenship. Patriotism is the highest duty of the democracy; you earn the vote by being prepared to lay down your life for your country. And when killed in war, the patriot is said to "pay the ultimate price."

So liberty—freedom from slavery, indenture and oppression—is a core democratic value. Although called free, it is priceless, which makes a curious contradiction with those free things that are of no value, like free stuff. How is it that the most high is also the lowest? These two senses of freedom—and their contradiction—are now driving a slow-motion train wreck through our lived experience of democracy.

Some people can't tolerate the contradiction. The white working class voter who voted for Donald Trump as the U.S. president, like the UK voter who chose to vote leave in the "Brexit" referendum on whether to end British membership of the European Union, struggled with the cost of a contradiction that is inherent in global social and economic change.

Donald Trump squared the circle for his followers when he "solved" the troubling contradiction of the Muslim patriot Captain Humayun Khan. A U.S. army officer, Khan died in Iraq in 2012. He gave his life; his parents too made the sacrifice. Their appearance at the 2016 Democratic rally for Hilary Clinton was about proving unity and social inclusion, since the Khans were Muslim.

While Khan's mother's grief was such that she could not bring herself to speak on the podium, Trump sneered at her as having nothing to say because she possibly "was not being allowed to speak." In this innuendo, Trump proposed that her religion outweighed her sacrifice as a citizen, and it allowed the anti-Muslim rhetoric of his campaign to go forward alongside the claim to defend the constitution and its freedoms.

This is a disgraceful politics by any measure, but particularly clear and cruel in the case of this mother's grief, for it implied that the sacrifice of her son, which she was obliged to make as a matter of law and citizenship, was somehow diminished by her religion giving her apparently a different class of citizenship.

She could not make the pure gift of the patriot mother, of her son to the nation. Despite her citizenship, and her sacrifice, Donald Trump suggested this gift was not really hers to give. It was a way of equivocating the value of the life given: this man could not be called a patriot, or be said to make the sacrifice, because he was Muslim. He hadn't paid since his life was not the appropriate currency; his ethnicity made of his gift an unwelcome one.

As philosopher Judith Butler argues in *Precarious Life*, some bodies are worth more than others—a point we can gauge by which bodies as a nation we are prepared to grieve. The contradiction that Trump toys with is the one in which the patriot, the purest symbol of the constitution, is a white man bearing arms to defend it. But in reality not all citizens are white men, and the reality of the modern armed forces is that not all patriots are white men, either, its membership including men and women of many creeds and cultures who fight as professional soldiers in theaters of war to which the government has varying degrees of commitment.

Trump went on to blame Hilary Clinton for the war in which Captain Khan was killed because she voted for it in the Senate. This is remarkable misogyny, attacking the mother and the woman nominee, and it conveniently overlooks that it was Republican president George W. Bush who initiated that war. But Trump achieved his rhetorical aim; in impugning Clinton for voting for it, Trump implied that if Iraq was an illegitimate war then its sacrifices do not count, and it was somehow his rival's fault that the patriot was neither white nor Christian.

Despite its cynicism, the repair Trump performed on the contradiction was enough to soothe his constituents temporarily until the next news cycle, and the caravan moved on. But it couldn't resolve this and the other paradoxes of recent global change that arise as contradictions for those living them. His attack on the Khans was cruel enough, but the deceit on his followers was crueler still since he exploited the pain of their contradiction to grab some free media time.

Change embodies contradiction simply in the way that it makes things otherwise than they were. A change for the better can be tolerated since no one complains when something is no longer as painful or laborious as it was. For a long time, technological change was change for the better of this sort, improving daily life and prosperity.

But two things now make contradiction more acute; the pace of change is accelerating, which means that more and more things are lost to the past. And the economics of technological change has intersected with globalization in a way that now sacrifices whole industries and communities. It narrows interests, and widens the gap between the beneficiaries and the dudded. More is lost and is lost more often.

It can be argued these changes now threaten to challenge the wellbeing of the nation in many places around the globe. But while the price of freedom may be eternal vigilance, it's not clear in what way bearing arms could defend us from the economics of technological change. It simply isn't that kind of threat.

THE FREE SAMPLE is not really free at all; as a marketing gambit, it is a claim on the shopper's attention. The free gift of a face cream distills the paradox: freedom is, at the same time, the highest democratic value, anchoring the political philosophy of modernity, and the giveaway of almost no value, inconsequential, something had "for free."

That the gift under discussion takes place in a department store is significant because it is within consumer culture that we find an answer to the question, "what is free?" The contradiction of the free gift converges on rhetorics of indebtedness and sacrifice, and moves *glissando* from department store to election hustings.

Nowhere is the revaluation of a value proposed by free stuff seen more clearly than in consumer logic, and yet nowhere is its challenge to the political more opaque. Is there even a relationship between the sense of freedom as a giveaway and the meaning of freedom as democratic keystone? Is it as Benveniste would have it that the two completely different senses can be harbored in the one signifier just because the meaning is clearly different in context? Is the homophony just an accident, as some philosophers of language would say, and therefore a circumstantial association? But isn't there, all the same and in virtue of it, the passage of leakage in significance, albeit unconscious, from one to the other?

# *[two]*

# *[free time]*

## welcome to the culture industry

OUR FREE TIME is neither free nor is it ours; instead it is a second channel for the endless economic contribution we must all make in the scheme of things. The creation of paid work has also created leisure, and now time is a commodity to be spent, on travel and culture, on overseas holidays and in art museums.

The promotional shot shows the cruise ship Carnival Freedom storming down the Grand Canal in Venice. Cruise ships from many cruise lines regularly sail in and out of Venice regardless of the damage done to the old city by the wash. There were 594 of them in 2018 alone.

Tourism is holding Venice captive. The city is staged for the benefit of holiday-makers as a life-size cultural theme park for well-heeled first-world culture vultures. It presents an enormous commodity of experiences—going on the "rides" (the gondolas & vaporetti), going to the various sights (Piazza San Marco, the island of Murano), buying the souvenirs (e.g., Murano glass). Venice is being inundated by its past, trapped as a giant cabinet of curiosities. Declares the mayor, "We must face it, Venice is not Disneyland—it is a real place where people live and work."

Modern cruise lines have replaced the nautical with the hospitality trope; the vessel is so large that rarely is bad weather felt, and indeed access to the outside, to the experience of the ocean, is severely restricted. This is unlike on older ships, where the miles of decks allowed for the reality of being at sea—the sensation of wind and waves—to penetrate. These days, you experience a vessel turned in on itself, the decks narrowed and "privatized" as balcony suites, while the interior of the ship becomes the experience—the shopping malls, the cafes, the theater shows—all increasing the exposure of the "guests" to opportunities to consume and to pay.

The cruise is a mode of tourism marketed as the peak of do-nothing luxury, in which lazing by the pool is punctuated by the eight-hour snapshots of exotic ports. The activity of sunbaking is emblematic of free time, according to the philosopher Theodor Adorno. Apart from being a way simply of doing nothing, he writes in "Free Time," it is also boring and uncomfortable.

Free time emerges from his essay as a source of painful reinforcement of our superfluity beyond the role assigned to us by productivity. Wage slavery has rendered us un-free and now the question of what to do with ourselves when not working has no satisfying answer.

In our free time, he imagines, we can merely contribute to the profits of the "leisure industry" by submitting to the inanity and boredom of camping or tourism; or to the disappointment of the pseudo-activity of the DIY project or other hobby in which our desire for expertise is mocked. The culture industry takes individual expression and dissects it into production and consumption, and those on either side of this divide find they are working for the system once again.

In Adorno's view, the culture industry infects everything with a kind of sameness. The impact of this sameness is an effect of it making economic all those activities that previously were outside it—the sociable, the pleasurable, the aesthetic, the amusing, those things from which we gained emotional and intellectual stimulation or refreshment, the things we found entertaining. Over the last century these pursuits have gradually been swallowed up by global cultural producers, and market imperatives have increasingly dictated what is available to us to do in our spare time.

Hollywood films, popular music, and package tours replace more local pleasures like reading books, going to the theater, having a sing-along around the piano, dancing or painting watercolors, and stamp collecting or woodwork, he imagines. Things we were inclined to do ourselves are now relinquished in favor of professionals creating entertainment with a more mass-produced finish. Like other industries, the culture industry is global and formulaic and it now threatens to cover the world with its algal bloom.

Boredom is the consequence of this indentured leisure, says Adorno: "Boredom is objective desperation." Beneath the dissatisfaction of not having enough to do, or of having nothing to stimulate and refresh us, lies an existential despair. It is trivialized by the stream of adjurations to purchase new experiences that all follow a similar formula so that it seems there is in effect no difference between the biennale cities of Venice, Sydney, Sao Paulo, or Gwangju.

## art vs tourism

VENICE IS FAMED for art and culture, and especially for its art biennale, held every second year and showcasing an exhausting array of contemporary art.

Fiona Hall's work for the Australian pavilion, "Wrong Way Time," at the 2015 Venice Biennale was modeled on the idea of the *wunderkammer*, the cabinet of curiosities. It made a fitting figure for the whole Biennale thing, and perhaps even for Venice itself in this present postmodern iteration as cruise boat destination. A biennale curates the place of the exhibition as much as the art itself. This is why it is called after the city where it is located. The capture of art by "experience," which is really of a particular kind of experience, fits with upscale tourism and the idea of curating a city as a theme park. The idea of the art biennale grew out of the trade fair, its brief to bring to the spectator an "experience" larger than the particular art works, displayed in a cornucopia of curation that extends to the city itself. Picturesque venues abound. Glorious experiences should be hard to avoid, moving through its exotic urban landscapes that come supplied with plenty of great food, good wine, and good coffee.

In practice, the leading experience is fatigue. The theme for the 2015 Venice Biennale promised "All The World's Futures." But *The Guardian*, for one, described it as "more of a glum trudge." Perhaps it's unsurprising, since contemporary art is now a creature of global commerce. "All the world" is united as a marketing opportunity to bring first-worlders to tourist venues. The repetition of themes about the future recently became uncanny. "The Future is Here—it is just not evenly distributed" was the theme taken for the 2016 Sydney Biennale. Or did this overlap in the themes and styles point to a broader exhaustion of the format? At last count, there were ninety-eight biennales or triennials in forty-eight countries.

Perhaps this is an effect of internationalizing art, which is really a homogenizing of it. Anything site-specific, of only local purpose and any sacred art, has been edited out long since. The biennale applies the same formula for spectacle to the different locations it colonizes. Is it any wonder that the art is beginning to look the same? The formula itself is engineering a future more daunting than bears contemplation—a monotony unrelieved by anything really different. While commodification is as old as capital, and an enduring source of indenture for artists, its effects are intensified by the global production of culture as a consumable. It initiates the production of the artist as a commodity at events like the Venice Biennale.

The Venice curation was divided into over-elaborate but obscure ideas. The curation guide told us that "All The World's Futures" was the intersection of three filters, “garden of lively disorders,” “of epic duration” and “reading capital.” In a field of metaphors, this last was literally meant—a reading of Marx’s tome took place at the Giardini daily.

The secret of the biennale form—art captured as commodity fetish—was hidden in plain sight. According to one magazine, the director of “Das Kapital the Oratorio” sauntered over to the Rolls-Royce tent for the after-party. The staging of the predicament of the culture industry having taken place, his work was done.

## the tourist vs the refugee

THERE WAS REALLY only one work at the Sydney biennale that seemed to fit the idea of an uneven distribution of the future directly, and that was an immersive video by Nilbar Güres, "Open Phone Booth," in which a woman sits atop arid mountains in Turkey trying to get a signal on her mobile phone.

But Turkey was an uncanny resonance. As the curator Stephanie Rosenthal noted in the guide to the exhibition, the "conditions of uneven distribution" are dictated by geopolitics and global economics, and she referred to the influx of political refugees "not just in Australia but internationally." In another work shown as part of the Sydney Biennale, French artist Céline Condorelli made a shining curtain from the foil-like material used in the thermal blankets that were elsewhere wrapped around refugees, pulled from their sinking boats at sea.

The Sydney curator's invocation of the rhetoric of immigration and the refugee had an ambivalent effect. It revived indirectly the ghost of the 2014 Sydney Biennale, in which a longstanding patron was forced to withdraw from the organizing committee because his company, Transfield, was involved in running controversial Australian offshore refugee camps. But this was already visible in the paucity of funds available, without the patron, to mount the show.

The buzz-word of the "refugee" allowed the curation "uneven futures" rhetoric to segue onto the structure of the exhibition, imagined we were told as clusters conceived of as "Embassies of thought." But, further reading of the curation in the guide revealed that

> they are explicitly not related to colonial or imperial history, diplomatic missions, cultural and linguistic boundaries, or capitalistic power structures . . . Instead, they provide safe spaces for thinking.

Actually, there is no embassy for the stateless; there is no safe space for the refugee, for thinking or for anything else. That is the point of the events unfolding in Europe and in Australia. Hannah Arendt of the Germany of the 1930s writes: "Denationalization became a powerful weapon of totalitarian politics. . . . The incredible plight of an ever-growing group of innocent people was like a practical demonstration of the totalitarian movements' cynical claims that no such thing as inalienable human rights existed."

We are told the global refugee crisis is now as bad as at any time since World War II. As the 2015 Venice Biennale progressed, large numbers of Syrian refugees were flooding out of Turkey and Greece and into the European Union. Trains from Venice to Munich were cancelled as the city was overwhelmed by the numbers coming from the south.

Nothing that was done really helped refugees at the biennales, either in Venice or in Sydney. Perhaps a curatorial essay is just hot air? If it is hard to put a finger on in what way Transfield tainted the Sydney Biennale with its financial interest in the holding camps, or Rolls-Royce slandered the Venice Biennale's "Reading Capital" with its after-party, it is because the way the culture industry takes up art products is complicated.

The profit interests behind the industry have been objectified in a kind of jargon that stands in for them in the art production. So for example, the jargon of "the embassy" is vacuous, yet uses the language of commitment. In using this language, and more generally the rhetoric of the "world's future," of geopolitics and displaced peoples, the curation of art around it emptied the refugee crisis of real meaning.

## dark tourism

THE ARTLESSNESS OF cultural tourism comes to something of a halt at Dachau. Literally, at the railway station called that, which is just one stop on a suburban Munich line. These days it's known as "dark tourism," the organized inspection of the sites of atrocities and tragedies.

In the wake of the Jewish holocaust, Hannah Arendt wrote, in *Eichmann in Jerusalem*, of the banality of evil. The concentration camp at Dachau is a terrible spectacle, not least because of the impermanent look of its buildings, the temporary and undistinguished huts in which hideous suffering was made commonplace. These places can hardly bear the weight of the scrutiny they must now receive from history. The most solid thing about Dachau seems to have been the motto, cast in iron, over the gate: "Work makes us free."

Bruno Bettelheim, in his book *The Informed Heart*, remembers the German Jewish people who could not leave behind their possessions and therefore remained to die in Nazi Germany: "My young relative was unable to convince some members of his family to go with him when he left . . . his family clung more desperately to the old living arrangements, the possessions they had accumulated over a lifetime. It was like a parallel process in which their life energies were drained away while their possessions seemed to give them a pseudo-security to replace the real assurance that no longer came from planning for their lives."

Bettelheim contrasts this response with the groups of others who, when they saw the writing on the wall, organized themselves into strategic positions in the SS, into political cells, into obtaining papers for emigration, and so on.

In exploring the psychology of the totalitarian society, and the mass society which shares features with it, Bettelheim concludes that changing the environment is a most effective way of changing personality. He finds this from his own experience of a radically changed environment, as an inmate of Buchenwald. Looking for an explanation of how the German people could have accepted the totalitarian tyranny of the Third Reich, he reflects on those victims of the Nazi state who perished under the weight of their earthly possessions. "Refugees fleeing the invading German armies were everywhere bogged down by the load of goods they carted in wagons, barrows, bicycles or on their backs, because they could not bring themselves to face life without them."

Bettelheim argues that, as citizens or as concentration camp inmates, ordinary people were all persecuted by the Nazis, for the aim of the totalitarian state was to deprive every individual of his autonomy, and to infantilize people by overriding their will to guarantee obedience. The structural difference between the camps and the larger society, in terms of this process of disintegration in the personality, was time: the concentration camp was faster-acting, because its terror and deprivation were more complete.

But the role of the concentration camp in the wider society was to posit a continuum with it. Whether or not Germans realized it consciously, the longer they lived under threat, the more energy it took to manage anxiety, and the less inner energy remained for the courage to act. "They were thrown back on externals that had formerly kept them going in times of stress." It is clear that this bondage of possessions was more than greed. These people were possessed by their possessions far more than they possessed them.

Perhaps the notion of property is more ambivalent than the confident assertion of ownership and control. The properties of things—the color of the curtains, no less than the strength of one's character—are bonded to each other in essential ways. They are imaginary bonds, but all the more compelling for arresting us in the order of the imaginary, which is the order of our identity. We speak of "having" possessions, but they can only be had psychically by taking them into our minds as an image. In the process of taking these things in, we can become as indentured to them as they to us.

In his book, Bettelheim expresses the hope that technology might free society for a relation to objects that is not lethal. He argues that technology has made possible the recognition that objects are far less vital to us than they used to be, "since it no longer takes a year's labor to acquire one good suit, or a good bed and mattress." But the environment must support this investment, or we can regress, as did the citizens of the Third Reich, to more infantile modes of possession.

The contradiction in modern consumer society is that, while the means to move beyond objects is more available than ever, the social world is more than ever invested in our relating to objects as commodities, consumption, and stuff. Our belonging to this world still leaves us vulnerable so that, were that bond to be ruptured, it would simply leave us as individuals outside imaginable, and therefore livable, life.

Sadly, while technological change may be testing the tensile strength of these imaginary bonds, that testing is not yet in the direction of a new way to relate to things as other than mental prosthetics.

## the action of the image

IN SEPTEMBER 2015, the image of the little drowned boy washing up on the beach from a sinking refugee boat in the Mediterranean cut through the negativity about refugees, calling out to others however incoherently. It produced a humanitarian outpouring from Europeans in response: “We will help!”

The image of the boy went viral, prompting opinion pieces to resound through the world’s press. Angela Merkel, responding to the previous shame of German history, invited the refugees to make their way to Germany for resettlement. Private citizens came down to the railway stations with food, clothes, and blankets for the arrivals.

Who orchestrated this exchange? The volunteers who massed at the stations or who drove vans of donated goods across the English Channel, putting aside racism in a rare generous impulse? The media who distributed the image worldwide, increasing their circulation but also the visibility of the crisis? Or the society who welcomed the refugees, as an addition to its already disadvantaged class of Arab guest-workers and incidentally as a pool of cheaper labor?

This photograph, going viral, showed us that the effects of the culture industry cannot seal off economic value from the action of the image. And these effects are not able to be completely predicted or controlled.

A recent artwork by Chinese artist Ai Weiwei presented a large-scale installation of a rubber dirigible like that used by refugees to make the precarious crossing of the Mediterranean. It was made from the same material and in the same factory that manufactures the very commodity. The boat, of an exaggerated length, was populated with human figures made in the same inflatable black rubber. Titled “Law of the Journey,” the boat was set among motifs printed around its plinth, quotable humanitarian sentiments from Kafka to Zadie Smith. Pun notwithstanding, this work was distressingly shallow.

Distressing because the refugee crisis is not shallow, and the statistic, that in 2017, 1 in 113 people on the planet is a refugee, is deeply distressing. So why did this work come across as glib? It was first exhibited in 2017 in Prague, at the Trade Fair Palace which was an assembly point for Jews before their deportation to the Terezín concentration camp in World War II. The Jewish holocaust created the case study of the stateless for modern politics.

But “Law of the Journey” implements the “one-size-fits-all” philosophy of globalization. Something about the syndicated nature of international art is encapsulated in the work, right down to the comment from Ai Weiwei about it (quoted in the Sydney Biennale guide): “There’s no refugee crisis, only a human crisis. . . . In dealing with refugees we've lost our very basic values. In this time of uncertainty, we need more tolerance, compassion, and trust for each other since we all are one. Otherwise, humanity will face an even bigger crisis."

Is it the art or the politics that is shallow? In presentations of international art, for example in biennales, it commonly seems taken for granted that a political angle is needed to tie the art together, but this is not a straightforward assumption. In general, the form supports the rise of work with a kind of stick-on protest, a global politics that is vaguely left-wing, vaguely green—but mostly vague, its action very imprecise.

This is because it isn't really about politics at all, but about sentiment. Why does this art presentation require a general political purpose? It's a marketing strategy, in which social value becomes cultural capital and thereby something that can be sold.

Ai Weiwei is now a brand. Persecuted by the Chinese government while he remained in Beijing, he is now living in exile in Berlin. His studio has been represented at various significant art fairs, collections and events since he was selected to represent China at the Venice Biennale in 1999. He has built a reputation for a kind of action art, and the political has been his material. He has been steadily becoming the quintessential international artist, a breed that is part citizen journalist, part NGO and part celebrity.

Ai developed his own idiom in the 1990s that, at its best, delivered art as a coup to the politics of domination. "Dropping a Han Dynasty Urn" (1995) spoke truth to power in the language of the objet d'art (not priceless but worth, as it happened, several thousand dollars).

An uncanny knack with vernacular objects, from military coats to school children's backpacks, and a vital engagement through social media, has created a style of political back chat that makes for activist art that is brilliantly laconic. But lately there have been missteps. The most awkward of these was the photo shoot that had him posing as the drowned three-year-old Kurdish boy washed up on the Mediterranean coast in 2015. This, and other images of Ai, has been billed as "drawing attention to the refugees' plight" on the shores of the Greek island Lesbos. But the image of Aylan Kurdi was already a protest, and Ai has been criticized for adding nothing to it but an artist's ego, attempting to insert himself between the tragedy and the lens.

Under the headline "A portrait of the artist as a dead boy," *Aljazeera* journalist Hamid Dabashi wrote: "You look at this picture of Ai Weiwei and you wonder: What does it exactly mean when a world renowned artist, a rather portly middle-aged man, poses as the malnourished dead body of a Syrian refugee child washed ashore as he and his family were trying to escape the slaughterhouse of their homeland?"

Dabashi diagnoses Ai's "epic fail" as a broader aesthetic malaise: "the fundamental failure of conceptual art as we know it today to come to terms with realities that have trespassed national, regional, or imaginative geographies of representation," he writes. What is this "crisis of artistic representation?" Does he mean a crisis for critique so that it can longer distinguish itself from the accidental image, on social media or in the press? Maybe the proliferation of the photographic, in photojournalism and advertising, has compromised the provenance of the art image so that we can no longer reliably see the difference.

The danger for a political artist like Ai Weiwei, who seeks to arrest the jargon of the globalizing world—in social media images of refugees, for example, to make it stand for something different—is like the tale of the insurance salesman and the priest attending him on his deathbed. The priest didn't succeed in converting the man to religion but he did come away insured.

## art vs marketing

IT IS SOMETIMES hard to distinguish where art ends and marketing begins. This is the global art market at work. The question that the current state of international art poses is: What is the difference between art and marketing?

Head of Art Business Studies at Sotheby's London Institute, Iain Robertson has described the art market as the effect of "consumerism, cultural nationalism and historicism," its momentum driven by the "economics of taste." This captures an uneven alloy of the desire of the rich for status trinkets, an avenue of money laundering, a commodity for speculation and the appreciation of national artworks.

The market is not necessarily anathema to art, but more than ever it directs it. And it deserves scrutiny because now it has become art itself. Can you see a difference between the glossy, brightly colored, witty, ecumenical-secular art images of global art biennales, the myriad Art Fairs held in every capital, the blockbusters at every museum seasonally in winter and summer, the annual round of contemporary art auctions at Sotheby—and the similarly glossy images offered as full-page feasts in magazines, online and on billboards, the store windows and movie clip advertisements everywhere? As Adorno and Horkheimer analyze it, "in the culture industry the subject matter itself, down to its smallest elements, springs from the same apparatus as the jargon into which it is absorbed."

This describes the problem in the recent trend to exhibitions of the big fashion brands, such as *Cartier: The Exhibition* (seen at the National Gallery of Australia, Canberra, in 2018), or *Dreams of Dior* (seen at the Victoria and Albert Museum, London, in 2019). It can be argued that Cartier is more than a brand, that its pieces of jewelry have their place in the history of fashion, craft, and the decorative arts. But such was the curation of the show, it emerged as an enormous free kick for the global conglomerate, Richemont, which in 2014 was the second-largest luxury goods company in the world after LVMH, and owning among other brands, Dunhill, Baume & Mercier, Montblanc, Piaget and Van Cleef & Arpels.

The Cartier show was a good example of art that "springs from the same apparatus as the jargon into which it is absorbed," since there was no critical appraisal of "brand" as art form, nor any interpretation of how the marketing economics directs the production of the work as it sets the scene for its exhibition. This is not to deny the obvious craftsmanship of the jewelry, but only to underline that a predicament that has faced the decorative arts throughout its history, and which held it down the pecking order below fine art, has now emerged as the condition of the art world as such.

Adorno and Horkheimer coined the phrase "the culture industry" more than sixty years ago. Since *The Dialectic of Enlightenment* was published, the concept of the culture industry is more prescient—and pressing—than it ever was. The idea of "jargon" is especially resonant, since it captures the constructing of art out of the ideological material of commerce without any distinction.

Adorno and Horkheimer had spent the war in exile in the United States, and had perhaps allowed apocalyptic thinking to overwhelm them. But they had developed an understanding of the intimacy developing between capital and politics. They describe a process by which style surmounts the work of art so that a kind of "seeming" comes to pass for art in the culture industry, while in fact undermining it. They write, "Being nothing other than style, [this art] divulges style's secret: obedience to the social hierarchy."

If they are right that style is the surrogate of the existing social system, then this would explain why, despite being positioned in a gallery, Cartier did not satisfy. It also captures the perverse boredom of biennales whose smooth curatorial gloss stifle the action of the individual pieces.

The *Dreams of Dior* exhibition shed more light on the question, and incidentally on the blockbuster as the genre that carries this collapse of art and market. As a design "event" it couldn't be faulted; the curation of the gowns dovetailed with the stories of their creation in ways that projected the necessity of the form. But on the subject of its material support—the market in haute couture that collaborates with the economic priorities of LVMH—it was silent. In this respect, it was only a more exaggerated display of the tropes that underwrite the blockbusters of Van Gogh, the Impressionists, the "masterpieces from the Hermitage" and so on. The market imperative on the galleries is to romance the paying public with the glamour of art. Dreams, indeed. That many of these exhibitions are devised to boost revenues in regional locations is not on display.

There was an enchanting room of dressmakers' toiles buried deep in *Dreams of Dior*. It served to romanticize these very conditions of production, much like how the story of Van Gogh's poverty or his madness pass for the "real story" in exhibitions featuring the sunflowers. The marketing is the raison d'etre, both for the consumer and the gallery.

## es arte

THE SILVER PONTOON could be seen from the launch going to and from Piazza San Marco. It was moored outside the municipal offices of the city of Venice.

"What is that?" I asked, expecting to hear that it had some role in waste disposal or refrigeration. "Es arte," the captain replied. It's art.

This pontoon, floating ambiguously on the lagoon, took the Biennale form by surprise. An object whose only function was to simulate function, it captured the essence of art. It showed that the Biennale formula gets art the wrong way round, as though it's all about the viewer. When in an important sense, art has never been just about gratifying the viewer, even when artists were indentured to wealthy princes and art's uses confined to display in churches and palaces, where function dictated its visual terms.

Creatively, wonderful art went somewhere else even under these constraints. And now, in the era of the artist-entrepreneur, art can still give us something we didn't know we were looking for—a satisfaction we don't master and can't purchase. Art always gives something away and for free. In our secular world, art is nearly the last place left where we might feel the commandment of something other than ourselves. It's the last antidote to the narcissism of marketing and end-user.

It shows us that the relation of the commodity to the work of art is complicated—the commodity is the converse of art, but it is also its epitome. It matters that art, although undeniably a satisfying experience, be something beyond entertainment. Otherwise, we will be stifled by our own manufactured desires and our massaged consumer expectations of getting what we want.

The culture industry does not provide new aesthetic forms. It imposes on techniques its external requirements, by which means economic function defeats aesthetic possibility. And the culture industry simultaneously engenders the regression required of us, as consumers and workers, to appreciate it and so to adapt to our position in the economic order.

But the pontoon showed me that things can still slip through the net.

THE IDEA OF free time is premised on a commodification of time, in which not all of our time is free. We spend our time in productive labor, contributing to a social structure as well as to the economic system. A link between free time, as leisure, and the appreciation of the arts, is paid as a kind of existential allowance to each of us under the "culture industry."

But this industry reserves the right not only to commodify our time but also our taste and finally, our perception of what is satisfying. These ideas, which are developed in Adorno and Horkheimer's work, come to life in figures of art and tourism, the itinerary of the cruise and the art biennale. The tourist finds a contrast in the figure of the refugee. They meet on the edge of the Mediterranean, in the city of Venice.

Here the influx of art lovers and tourists threaten to swamp the city, which has itself become reinvented as a commodity. At the same time, the region is swamped by a different tide—of refugees seeking a better life in the "first world." The difference between the journey of tourists on their cruises and refugees in their inflatable boats can hardly be more stark.

Derrida's strictures on the history of capital in *Spectres of Marx* were pitted against the aestheticizing of the philosophy, in a performance of "Das Capital: the Oratorio" at the 2015 Venice Biennale. The Biennale reached out to the currency of this issue of geopolitical concern, but served only to reissue it as a promissory note in the banalizing grip of the culture industry.

# *[three]*

# *[free market]*

## art vs marketing II

AN ANECDOTE TOLD of Andy Warhol offers an illustration of how marketing adds value: as a tribute, Warhol presented Greta Garbo, an idol of his, with a drawing of a butterfly he had made. But she, apparently unimpressed, took a look then screwed it up and threw it on the ground. He picked it up, smoothed it out and wrote on it in a gesture that simultaneously neutralized the insult and co-opted the celebrity: "Crumpled Butterfly by Greta Garbo."

Andy Warhol's drawings of shoes featured in advertisements in *The New York Times* for a decade before he made his famous pop images. Warhol was careful to build his brand; from his early days as an illustrator for Madison Avenue, he created the disheveled boyish image of Raggedy Andy, being sure to mess up his clothes that were bought nevertheless from upscale Brookes Bros. He well understood the love of brands, and their role as totems in the modern mythology of American consumer life in the mid-twentieth century.

As he made his reputation, he began signing many of his illustrations for ads, understanding instinctively that what he was producing in his signature was a brand. But of course the signature was also the imprimatur of a fine artist, and in this pretension he issued a challenge to the distinction observed, then as now, between fine art and commercial art.

In pop art, the public was shown a veneer; Warhol as a prefabricated surface of this marketing life. Brands like Coca-Cola, packaging for ubiquitous everyday products like Campbell's Soup and Brillo, and celebrities similarly packaged in the masks afforded by the publicity shot, were rendered on the inscrutable surface of screen printing.

The Warhol we encounter before pop is a very different creature; loving, tender, playful. A diligent craftsman, a gifted draftsman. While pop was inscrutable, advertising was beguiling; the dainty, witty, confiding illustrations of shoes, bags, girls, and flowers keep company with stylized fingers and piano keys, mythical and household objects, and a multitude of shoes. Warhol the adman was all charm: he won several Art Directors Club awards during the 1950s.

The place of repetition in Warhol's early commercial work, as seen in the "Happy Butterfly Day" illustrations (1955) among others, set up the larger question of the reproduction in art, which would later take over his canvasses with soup cans and coke bottles. All this could pass as deadpan reproduction, the advertiser's style without substance, except for the knowingness of seriality—the giddying arrays of soup cans or electric chairs were given the same treatment as Elvis and Jackie Onassis, and spoke to the infinite regress of mass production and mass media.

Warhol made sure to get rich before turning to fine art. Was this biting the hand that fed, or perhaps fattening the cow for slaughter? Pop was more than ambivalent iconoclasm, and it wasn't just the tearing down of high abstraction by those who paid the piper. The opposition that delineated fine art and commercial art was highly vulnerable by the mid-twentieth century because all art had become a commodity. Thus Warhol also queered art by crashing the commercial world into the art world and installing marketing as the new mechanism of it.

Brand Warhol was the epitome of avant-garde style at the same time as it hollowed out the work, reducing it to a signature. It was the frank disclosure of art as a commodity like any other, like the shoes and bags of Fifth Avenue and like the poses of cherished celebrities and the look of famous brands.

So revealing a deeper truth about Warhol as a figure of modern art; he heralded the capture of art by marketing. All artists are commercial artists, he said, in that they sell their work to live. "Pop" was the biggest crisis in fine art of the twentieth century, the apostasy in which canvas was reduced to billboard. Or was it the most devastating critique? Certainly after Warhol's screen prints of Campbell's Soup and Marilyn Monroe, abstract painting was no longer the unrivaled medium of fine art. At the same time, Warhol took away the possibility of the distinction. In an Emperor's New Clothes moment, the difference between fine art and commercial art collapsed and with it the old pretension of art for art's sake.

Blockbusters are now the bread-and-butter of galleries and museums the world over. The principle of these shows—taking prime space in the local gallery and charging a hefty entry fee for locals to see it—seems at best to have an art educational rationale. At its most cynical, it provides critical revenue for public galleries that nowadays need to justify what they do in terms of its market appeal.

Ai Weiwei was billed alongside Andy Warhol in a blockbuster in the 2016 Andy Warhol/Ai Weiwei at the Warhol Museum, Pittsburgh. (It transferred from the National Gallery of Victoria, Melbourne). The show featured, among other things, the well-known Warhol screen prints of Chairman Mao from 1972. Mao is presented as a celebrity in two-dimensional graphic art, a style Warhol also used for Elvis Presley, Marilyn Monroe, and other cultural icons. The works project an uncanny prescience about the direction of political fame and the blurring of politics and marketing that peaks today in fake news and social media.

How could one make the vector of globalization and the art world more pointed? Every aesthetic resource in the images is recruited to it—the flat plane, the resonance of commercial art, the scale of celebrity, and its reduction to the image. Alive and disturbing, the repetitive array is reprised today as Xi Jinping (or as Kim Jong-un) taking the photo-op with Donald Trump on reality TV. These works remain a deft condensation of the *zeitgeist* of the art vs. marketing image; the action has intensified rather than fallen away.

Art now not only takes place in the market, but it takes place as the market. It is a challenge to find the medium through which today one can escape this logic. The constant cycling of provocation, and its recycling as co-opted pitch, characterizes the struggle of art globally in the marketing age.

## massaging democracy

IN ROLAND BARTHES' essay on "Soap Powders and Detergents," he points up how cleverly marketing can work to solicit us to buy by appealing on psychological levels.

He writes of how we can usefully contrast "the psycho-analysis of purifying fluids (chlorinated, for example) with that of soap powders (Lux, Persil) or that of detergents (Omo)" in terms of the relations they evoke "between the evil and the cure, between dirt and a given product."

> Chlorinated fluids, for instance, have always been experienced as a sort of liquid fire . . . The implicit legend of this type of product rests on the idea of a violent, abrasive modification of matter: the connotations are of a chemical or mutilating type: the product "kills" the dirt. Powders, on the contrary, are separating agents: their ideal role is to liberate the object from its circumstantial imperfection: dirt is "forced out" and no longer killed. (1972, 35)

But in addition, advertisements based on psychology can be contrasted with those based on psychoanalysis—"Persil Whiteness" for instance, "bases its prestige on the evidence of a result; it calls into play vanity, a social concern with appearances," whereas advertisements for Omo "chiefly reveal its mode of action"; involving the consumer "in a kind of direct experience of the substance, make him the accomplice of a liberation rather than the mere beneficiary of a result."

In this way, the marketing insinuates something of the psyche in the purchaser—the passion of cleanliness through fire or inundation through water—into the product. The deep orientations of fear, loathing, contempt, and disgust, the projection of shame and abjection and defenses against it—are projected onto the consumer choice for cleaning products.

This is the whole premise of marketing, that it is possible to influence people's actions through moving their desires by applying certain kinds of psychic pressure, often through presentation of certain images. The realm of human emotions is about the meeting of others through recognition as the source of emotional satisfaction. But manipulation is the opposite of recognition, and in everyday use, it depletes the human in much the same way as do other versions of the instrumental.

According to Wikipedia, "Marketing is the study and management of exchange relationships." This seems a succinct formula of the phenomenon which is among the most developed instances of instrumental reasoning.

On its website, the American Marketing Association offers its own version of social benefit: "From a societal point of view, marketing provides the link between a society's material requirements and its economic patterns of response. This way marketing satisfies these needs and wants through the development of exchange processes and the building of long-term relationships." This gloss is itself a creation of marketing, projecting itself as a necessary but neutral intermediary that accomplishes satisfaction for all concerned while "virtue-signaling" around goods like long-term relationships. But there has been an awareness since early in its development that marketing relies on a kind of management that moves from rhetorical message to manipulation.

Much is made in some readings of the fact that Edward L. Bernays, "the Father of Public Relations," was the nephew of Sigmund Freud. In the 2002 BBC documentary "The Century of the Self," presenter Adam Curtis comes close to blaming Freud for the rise of marketing: in episode one, Curtis refers to "how those in power have used Freud's theories to try and control the dangerous crowd in an age of mass democracy."

Curtis' imputation of a mob behind the concept of democracy picks up Bernays' own frank evaluation of "the masses." The value is closer to that critiqued by Arendt as totalitarian. He wrote in his 1928 book, *Propaganda*:

> The conscious and intelligent manipulation of the organized habits and opinions of the masses is an important element in democratic society. Those who manipulate this unseen mechanism of society constitute an invisible government which is the true ruling power of our country. . . . We are governed, our minds are molded, our tastes formed, our ideas suggested, largely by men we have never heard of. This is a logical result of the way in which our democratic society is organized. Vast numbers of human beings must cooperate in this manner if they are to live together as a smoothly functioning society. . . . In almost every act of our daily lives, whether in the sphere of politics or business, in our social conduct or our ethical thinking, we are dominated by the relatively small number of persons . . . who understand the mental processes and social patterns of the masses. It is they who pull the wires which control the public mind. (1928, 9–10)

In Arendt's 1946 essay "The Image of Hell," she describes how propaganda creates a fictitious world that destroys common sense. As Diprose and Ziarek distill it, Arendt concludes that the forms of totalitarian organization "are designed to translate the propaganda lies of the movement, woven around a central fiction—the conspiracy of the Jews, or the Trotskyites, or 300 families, and so on—into a functioning reality, to build up, even under non-totalitarian circumstances, a society whose members act and react according to the rules of a fictitious world" (2018, 141). The fictitious world is fabricated by "techniques and technicians of propaganda"—the marketers of the movement, no less.

Of course marketing, it will be said, is a hired gun—this is the bald extent of its instrumentalism, that it can promote public health as easily as racist division.

## market sentiments

IN ARTIST HELEN Grace's photo-work "Sleep Per Night—April–December 2008," minutes of sleep are plotted against days of the month, overlaid on a sepia photograph of the trading floor of the Chicago Board of Trade. The "bio-data" is generated from the artist's own diaries from the time, which was a time of sleepless nights for investors at the advent of the Global Financial Crisis.

In the analysis of financial markets, graphs make changing moods and emotional states into empirical realities via the logic of the "candlestick" chart, a stock in trade of "technical analysis." Traders use technical analysis to decide whether to buy, sell or hold. In the candlestick chart, the movement of the price, not merely its position, can be seen on inspection, highlighting trends. The candlestick method of charting was developed in the eighteenth century by Japanese rice traders, Grace tells us, but is now widely used to depict securities, derivatives, and currency movements.

The trend is a trajectory across time. It can create the illusion of seeing the future. It may promise to alleviate risk. Yet the direction is a mirage, never quite capturing the moment at which the traders run to the other side of the ship. The underlying shales of the stock market expose us to "market sentiments." The mad empiricism of the global markets is where market sentiments collect together the fugitive and irrational moments of investor behavior and spin it into objective fact.

As seen in the Global Financial Crisis, these sentiments can be unvarnished. And, because of the international nature of electronic investment, the local market is subject to global "market risk." This may have little to do with the viability of listed companies on individual exchanges as measured by, for example, price to earnings ratios. Despite the language of "rationalisation," "economic rationalism," and so on, the market can't be relied on to be rational—business journalist Alan Kohler has described a volatile afternoon through the unfolding of the Global Financial Crisis as traders acting "like kids on red cordial."

The frightening paradox of the market is that, for all it is presented as a blind force of indefeasible calculation—even of rationalism—it is dominated by the notion of its moods. "Investor sentiment," "business confidence," the twin antimonies of fear and greed: while economics is a science for pessimists, the market is a place of pragmatists betting on other people's feelings.

Grace reflects on another action of the market, the speculation on the future of necessary commodities. Graphs are suspended over photographs of Asian workers in the paddy fields, provoking the insight that production is built on (someone else's) labor. These charts call to mind the havoc wrought on third world staples by the global market. Speculation on the future of crops is also betting for or against starvation, a real anxiety given by drought and loss of land for edible crop planting.

In her catalog essay, Grace also asks us to speculate on "What happens when the private individual goes public, floating himself or herself into the stream of risky capital flows?" Is this fantasy—or is it Facebook? Social media, the sites where people perform themselves "for fun and profit," make the question urgent. "How do we survive in a market-dominated world, which devalues and discounts life and labour? What prospects currently exist for maximising returns on a public offering of the individual body and its emotional states?" she writes. That remains to be seen.

The bar graph becomes a simple and forceful presentation of the difficulty of living the crisis, where everyone has something on the (bottom) line. Thus, in the larger work in which these images appear, Grace's series of "bio-data sets" chart not only sleep per night, but "general anxiety," "state of happiness," "sense of security and belonging" and "filial sentiment" for the period, generating a self-portrait with cerebral intent.

In presenting her own emotional life as a kind of data the market could use, Grace performs a significant condensation: the impossible vagaries of individual mood are transposed onto the attempt of the market to leverage collectivized mood in its movement. It is of course a feedback loop; the more consumer sentiment lags, the more economic performance drags. "Everywhere you turn and on every surface and screen, there are images of beautiful figures, lines rising ever skyward and cloudless blue skies promising infinite growth, security, and high return. It seems that economics itself is a sublime landscape, while at the same time, art is merely another asset class."

Helen Grace's graphs show pattern recognition to be an aesthetic form. The creative power of facts and figures, through being visualized, produce value as much as record it. Strangely, the increasing visualization of the markets in charting coincides with the disappearance of visual drama from stock market trading floors. It's all gone digital. In the same way, we ourselves are "dematerialized" from physical forms to data flows, in the speculation on our wants and needs.

## real estate

WE PORE OVER the real estate pages because, for most of us, the house that we own is our major asset. It has been a deliberate strategy of postwar governments to distribute wealth "democratically" by allowing ordinary people to purchase their homes using mortgages rather than to rent perpetually from already-existing property owners.

Maybe it's salutary that U.S. President Donald Trump is a New York realtor. The power of property to generate wealth has moved dramatically with the course of modern democracy. In the days when land ownership was concentrated in the hands of the aristocracy, the average person belonged more to the land than it belonged to them. But property has now taken on the features of the commercial world of commodities at the same time as it has continued to operate as an essential place for human community.

The commodification of the human need for shelter is a negative consequence of creating property as an asset. The ability to be settled in a neighborhood, in a community that you have ties with, perhaps across generations, is undermined when speculation in the residential property market takes prices out of reach of those who live there.

The Marxian slogan "property is theft" refers to this privatizing of the whole world. "Exclusive possession" literally deprives others of space. Residential property dressed up as an asset class takes something for one group of people at the expense of others. We have already driven many species of animals from their space—we call it "habitat destruction." In the privatizing of property and the commodification of home and shelter, we have an intimidating challenge to the wellbeing of people now and to come.

Consider the Global Financial Crisis. The making of the human need for shelter and the social value of "home" into something that is bought and sold became the origin of the problem underpinning the "sub-prime mortgage."

In mortgage lenders Freddie Mac and Fanny Mae, the U.S. government had been extending to low and middle income citizens the privileged security and wealth-building vehicle that property ownership affords while offering an investment vehicle to the market. Originating with Roosevelt's New Deal, this was not a socialist aim so much as an effort to expand the pool of stakeholders in this market and perhaps in the whole idea of a market. The circle of society with a stake in the financial strength of the market would theoretically be increased and the number of adherents to the capitalist economic ideology would be expanded. (The same logic has been behind the expansion of the pool of investors to include "Mums & Dads" through compulsory superannuation).

There was no doubt also the hope that bringing working people into the status of home ownership would result in more wealth being generated through appreciation, which would in turn generate greater consumption by ordinary people fueling more jobs and more economic growth in the classic feedback loop of a free market system. And so it did for a time. The principle is illustrated in the converse; in the statistic that it was the middle percentage of the U.S. population who lost most as a result of the GFC—the very poor were only 20 percent poorer but the middle class lost over 50 percent on average of their wealth. Part of the U.S. population were literally living on borrowed time, as the expansion of the means to home ownership increased demand for property and predictably caused a housing bubble.

But the aggravation of the risk into a full-blown crisis—one that threatened the entire global financial system, and the real economies of the developed and developing world that underwrote it—came about because of speculation in various derivatives on mortgages; in effect, on the property market itself. This was brought about by the abstracting of the share market from real instruments to speculative instruments that in many ways were a species of gambling. In 2003, Warren Buffet likened derivatives to weapons of mass destruction. Derivatives revealed that there is an element in financial speculation that is nothing more than betting on the probability of future outcomes. The fact that it went so horribly wrong shows that probability is not a perfect measure of the future.

In the wake of the collapse of these towers of credit, the market froze, paralyzed by a loss of trust and so of liquidity and the visible risk opened up like a chasm. It forced the market back on itself in the "paradox of thrift," producing recession.

It was the intersection between the rampant greed of professional speculation, poorly regulated, colliding with the desires of people to secure wealth and security of tenure for themselves and their families, that created this perfect storm. What was being bartered in making residential property into a vehicle of speculation was the mode of life of ordinary people. It became subjected to the market and a creature of its speculation. The fear of insecurity and the desire for security contributed to the boom-bust cycle. Meanwhile, the derivative instruments built on over-optimistic, and in many cases deceptive, fascia put around them as "credit ratings" were too good to be true, and papered over the risk that was grouped together in those assets.

The failure of forecasting and regulation to foretell this destructive spiral only serves to underline the lack of rationality in an apparently rational system. There was a contradiction in the idea of the free market. In theory, it promised to smooth out supply and demand with the hum of a well-oiled machine. Instead, the free market became more like a monstrous behemoth that could roll over whole national economies and destroy cherished structures of financial security if left to its own devices. The events of the GFC laid bare the horrible reality that the free market does not necessarily regulate itself in the way anticipated by its optimistic proponents, that is, in the direction of equilibrium and to maximize prosperity.

Like the state of nature, the free market presented a freedom to be feared. The Global Financial Crisis was salutary in representing a peculiarly technological danger in the market; the excess of an instrumental reason unchecked by other intelligence. It was the exponential progression of the crisis, from a predicament rooted in land—literally concretized in the fabled territory of Middle America—to the vertiginous expanses of a digital globalization, which was yoked by a string of electronic vistas to the guts of the world economic system.

And yet, as Jon Roffe has written in *Abstract Market Theory*, the crisis was all the more fearful for not being outside the idea of the market. "[U]rgent questions about the market certainly arose in public discourse. The apocalyptic tone of these questions is unmissable: Is capitalism over? Has the market brought about its own collapse? Will the crisis and its effects ever really end?" But, as he goes on to argue:

> Both the very real catastrophe and the furious enunciations of our legion of post-hoc harbingers should not lead us to overlook its most important lesson: that there was no crisis for the market itself. What was and remains true is simply that the market continues to work. The abject failure of certain practices and their horrifying downstream effects should not distract us from its uninterrupted functioning. (2015, 2)

## worshipping mammon

IT TURNS OUT that capitalism is a kind of religion. It is not so much that Capital is a deity, as that it is the beneficiary of that supernatural belief in a time without creed but still in the thrall of superstition.

For Agamben, this abstracting of value to its pure symbolic form came on an empirical date—August 15, 1971—when the President of the United States unshackled the dollar from the gold standard. Henceforth, value was pure self-supporting abstraction; a metaphysical regression had befallen the previously earthly tool of mammon. Money was hypostasized, and evolved from the contrast with the ideal to become its icon. The material became immaterial.

The world economy did not collapse then and there—indeed, its resilience showed that value was generated purely out of differentials and had no need of a material guarantee. But in ascending into heaven in this way, the dollar showed that Capital was the heir to the spiritual deity and specifically to its power of judgment. This is why economists could mistake the action of the market for a kind of governance, and the setting of price for the defining production of value.

Drawing on Weber's figuration of the place of Protestantism in the origins of capitalism, Agamben outlined the metaphysical underpinning of political economy. But economics, capital in the form of the market, cannot usurp the political space without banishing the human scale. Where the market supplants other forms of judgment, capital directs democracy, and economics takes over politics, a kind of rationalization (to use Weber's term) risks turning the market relation into a form of oppression.

Agamben lays out this argument in part five of *Creation and Anarchy*—he writes that the de-materializing of money had an historical index on August 15, 1971 when "the American government, under the presidency of Richard Nixon, declared that the convertibility of the dollar into gold was suspended. . . . Although this declaration *de facto* marked the end of a system that long bound the value of money to a gold base, the news, which arrived at the height of the summer holidays, received less discussion then it would have been legitimate to expect" (2019, 66).

But this process of "money's de-materialization" had begun centuries before with the introduction of paper money as a substitute for metallic value, so the change had been coming for awhile. The argument had developed already from Schumpeter in the nineteenth century, Agamben tells us, who reflected that "all money is only credit" after all.

After August 15, 1971, money is a credit "that is founded solely on itself and that it does not correspond to anything but itself." Money has been abstracted; "evacuated of any value that is not purely self-referential."

There is something akin to transubstantiation in this moment of the decoupling of money and the gold standard. To explore it, Agamben goes via an argument of Walter Benjamin's about capitalism as a kind of religion (the argument is taken from fragment 74 in his collected writings). There had previously been a recognition by Carl Schmitt and others, that socialism was the new religion for the nineteenth and twentieth centuries, occupying the same place in psychosocial schemas as Christianity had held two millennia before. Now capitalism, too, could be seen in its aspect as a psychosocial investment, dramatized by the American ideology that funded the Cold War.

"According to Benjamin, capitalism does not represent only, as in Weber, a secularization of the Protestant faith, but is itself essentially a religious phenomenon." It develops its psychosocial positioning along the lines sketched in Nietzsche's argument in the *Genealogy of Morals*.

Benjamin develops an apocalyptic line of thought in which capital is not merely the heir of Christianity, but a transformation that intensifies the psychic deformation Nietzsche imagines taking place in the human psyche as a result of the invention of guilt and credit. Indeed, Benjamin describes capitalism as "a permanent and extreme cult," in which all hope of redemption has been removed. It is the first instance of a cult that *creates* guilt (that is, debt), and not atonement.

Writes Agamben: "Precisely because it tends with all its might not toward redemption but toward guilt, not toward hope but toward desperation, capitalism as a religion does not aim at the transformation of the world but its destruction." And the conviction that it holds over our own time is so complete that "even the three great prophets of modernity (Nietzsche, Marx and Freud) conspire with it, according to Benjamin, and are somehow in solidarity with the religion of desperation" (2019, 68). This dramatic argument finds capitalism to be both the economic isomorph to totalitarianism and the psychosocial incarnation of the death drive.

Benjamin's argument is given credit in Agamben from its excavation of the Greek word *pistis*. The term used in the New Testament by Jesus and the apostles to mean "faith" is the same word in modern Greek for "credit" (as in *trapeze tes pisteos*, or Bank of Credit.) Faith "is simply the credit we enjoy with God and the Word of God enjoys with us when we believe or credit him."

"Capitalism is a religion entirely founded on faith; it is a religion whose adherents live *sola fide*, by faith alone. And just as according to Benjamin, capitalism is a religion in which the cult has been emancipated from every object and guilt from every sin, thus from every possible redemption, so too, from the point of view of faith, does capitalism have no object: it believes in the pure fact of believing, in pure credit, which is to say, in money."

The Nixon decision of 1971 therefore ratifies the principal underlying the whole show—it functions like "a clarification of its own theological content comparable to Moses['s] destruction of the golden calf." The doctrine we might say of capital "now emancipates itself from any external referent, cancels its idolatrous connection with gold, and affirms itself in its absoluteness. Credit is a purely immaterial being."

Agamben observes that this de-materialization removes "the final obstacle to the creation of a money market, to the complete translation of money into a commodity" (2019, 70). A metaphysics of the market is now expressed: "a society whose religion is credit which only believes in belief is condemned to live on credit."

Cue the Global Financial Crisis.

## price vs value

IF, AS ROFFE suggests, the Global Financial Crisis was not a crisis for the market, what does this tell us?

Perhaps, most clearly, that the market is not a method of governance. When right wing economic pundits recommend we "leave it to the market" to sort out, they imagine they are appealing to a force somewhere between God and rough justice.

The market is an instrument for setting price, and so the market is a generic device for the production of value. More than that, it is itself a creature of value. It instantiates a mode of the production of value, and the value that it sets in train is not hypothetical. It produces a way of being in the world. In terms of life calibrated this way, value is generated as price in the prism of the market.

Economists' definition of value raises the question to what extent price measures the value of anything that one person has that another person wants. But value is seen as a knife on its edge in this example. If we turn the blade to see its flat surface, we understand a great deal more about the knife. Inside the optic of price and the market, certain things are flattened that in reality have dimension. Value arises all the time and everywhere, and its production is not a mystery close up but an empirical actuality lived as something we are familiar with.

As Weber described in *Economy & Society*: "The market community as such is the most impersonal relationship of practical life into which humans can enter with one another" (1968, 636). A real estate market shows the changing of value depending on social nuances of time and space, taking an itinerary around the resources of the shelter and *habitus*. Value is not a mystery, although it is at every moment a matter of empirical calculus. The example of real estate presents a phenomenology of value; in experience, value is highly striated, highly textured, highly contextualized, and it grows as an empirical event out of a web of practices. Its abstraction in the idea of its price is an oversimplification, and an impoverishment of lived experience.

That intuition is not approachable through brute economics. Instead it calls for a theoretical elaboration through a kind of convergence, the evolving of previously distinct concepts into a common task and a single device.

The market is not the only locus for the production of value, but it is in globalization a dominant one, and its operation shows that more than price is generated. It is a potent source of value production in society; it creates around it layers of meaning, and initiates material circumstances including political circumstances.

Markets are almost pure forms of the instrumental; and their dominance brings to life the subordination of the political to the economic that Arendt foresaw in *The Human Condition*. The reduction of value to price is the same conceptual reduction that we see in other instrumental thinking. But perhaps in the market, it is at its most convincing and most stark: the stripping away of the nuance and the flattening of purposes into the pinpoint of a numerical value.

MARKET CREATES VALUE by setting price. It eclipses other ways of producing value, other ways of bringing to visibility kinds of value in human living.

The market is a machine for producing value, a machine specifically that produces value as price. The thinking that gives us the free market is expressed in the mysterious adequation between price and value, which in economic rationalism becomes a distinction without a difference. But while price is a creature of the market (and an expression of the tension between supply and demand), value spills out beyond the market into the three-dimensional world of social meaning.

This machinic quality of the market allies it with the technological era that we inhabit, as it does with the entities of commodity and bureaucracy which are also concepts proper to the technological. That argument—from commodity to bureaucracy to market—forms an arc that displays each as species of instrumental reasoning. Technology is its end term which applies instrumental thought.

We have come to this through considering symptoms of freedom. When we see the revaluation of a value, in for example, the going from the highest democratic value to the zero price gambit, then a process of change is evident. The direction of conceptual change can be observed in the flipping of the free from democracy to free stuff.

What is allowing this instrumentalism to take hold as an agent of change? And why the totalizing habit of this instrumentalism? It throws up the paradox of a totalitarian constraint inside a free market world. The becoming-economic of the political—the free market producing value in terms of price—is that form of instrumentalism that observes the political being absorbed into the economic.

Marketing is the tendentious undertow in representations of the state of inter/national affairs that are increasingly economic. But while presented as self-evidently factual, and even as an independent reality that cannot be resisted, the market is a construct whose premise is desire and whose movement is based on sentiment.

Critique moves through the democratizing of wealth as evidenced in real estate and home mortgages, to the catastrophic losses of the Global Financial Crisis and its underlying causes in a commodification of the need for shelter and a speculation derived from it, literally in financial derivatives. The appearance of the market as a rational means of value production, its attendant "science of persuasion," marketing, and the imperative of its offshoots like the "business model," present themselves as self-evident, which is a sure sign of their metaphysical origin.

# *[four]*

# *[free speech]*

THE DECLARATION OF "post-truth" as the 2016 word of the year hailed an extraordinary, some would say preposterous, change in the conduct of political discourse.

We might have expected a contest over political truth. But over the plain truth as shown in photographs? When a CNN interviewer queried the size of the crowd at the Trump inauguration, advisor Kelly Ann Conway denied the numbers were smaller than those for Obama several years earlier, despite the evidence.

She referred instead to the president's use of an "alternative fact" in his claim the crowds were the largest ever. Said the CNN interviewer: "Isn't an alternative fact a falsehood?"

"Comment is free but facts are sacred," wrote the editor of *The Guardian* in 1921. The slogan appears over the comment page on the paper's website. But the *Oxford Dictionary* defined post-truth as: "relating to or denoting circumstances in which objective facts are less influential in shaping public opinion than appeals to emotion and personal belief."

As the dictionary noted, the word had been increasingly in circulation in the lead up to Brexit and to Donald Trump's presidential nomination. It was "fuelled by the rise of social media as a news source and a growing distrust of facts offered up by the establishment." Post-truth enters the lexicon as a function of the rise of populist politics in the United States and Europe.

There is irony in a dictionary, repository of reference, and a source of authority for the truth of meaning, adding a word like "post-truth" to its lexicon. And the term entered originally as irony it seems—in reporting this, *The Guardian* referred to the dictionary's citation that the first time the term "post-truth" was used was in a 1992 essay by Serbian American playwright Steve Tesich in *Nation* magazine. Tesich, writing about the Iran-Contra scandal and the Persian Gulf war, said that "we, as a free people, have freely decided that we want to live in some post-truth world."

Careless speech, ignorant speech, outrageous speech and outright lies were previously the province of the alt-right fringe, but what was shocking in 2016 was its move into the mainstream of political language. But living in a time of acute fragmentation of perspectives, or even in a time of extreme manipulation of popular opinion, is not the same thing as being in an era when nothing is true. Some things can't perhaps be determined to be truth or lies, as corresponding to anything, because they apply to future events. The rhetoric of Trump and other political promises has traded on this.

The predicament that Trump put to his audience was the anxiety that he would not keep his promises against the anxiety that he would. If we are post-truth, so that the politician's promise is not the point—"he only said that stuff to get elected," as businessman Gerry Harvey put it following 2016 U.S. Election Day—then what is the point of the genre? The chaos imagined to be unleashed by a politician shamelessly foisting the world of post-truth on the public discourse has caused great outcry. And yet, perhaps, greater outcry at the possibility when he did move to keep promises—to ban Muslims, to build a wall with Mexico, etc.

There was a breach of trust in bank bailouts and imposed austerity measures for the democratic citizens of many countries in the wake of the GFC, forced to pay as they saw it for the speculative excesses of elites. Post-truth became a proxy for the fear that "you will never know the truth," as in "they will deceive you," "they" will keep it from you, and will deny the self-evident. Post-truth is a proxy for the fear of being deceived and for the conviction that, whatever they say, you will be made to pay. This is because politicians lie, even the most plausible of them, and even the ones you are inclined to trust.

President Obama came to be regarded as one of these. The misfortune for Obama was that, for all his inclusive eloquence, history gave him the task of putting a radically inequitable financial system on taxpayer-funded life support within weeks of inauguration. His slogan of "Yes we can," his message of hope, was trashed in this bailout of the banks in the global financial crisis, however much that action was defensible and even essential in terms of "saving the world" from itself.

It probably wouldn't have worked to let the banks fail; it certainly would have inaugurated a post-capitalist moment in which apocalypse would be visited hardest on ordinary working folk. But because the bullet was dodged, nobody gave credit for the precipice that the free world had been coaxed back from, and all they could see then was what they had lost. The jobs, the houses, the savings. Obama was mugged by reality. His legacy might be regarded as one in which the hazards of political rhetoric met the corruption of the real world in a head-on collision. While he succeeded in saving the furniture, he didn't get to abolish inequality as his rhetoric had promised. If Obama had a problem, it was that he was too good a speaker. His oratory, however sincere, now suffers from the taint of sophistry. And then, it might also be said, his silences suffered from too much tact. What he didn't say did the damage as well as what he did.

Trump, as the reality-TV president, was the paradoxical beneficiary of public disenchantment. The voters punished Obama not with a vote for a more moderate ambition but with a leap into magical thinking. Possibly the outright fraud of the GFC and its aftermath is in large part responsible for the hollowing-out of faith in truth, fact and public discourse. Ordinary citizens paid for the excess of finance—in Greece, in the U.S. rust-belt, in the north of England—and saw they were picking up the tab for others richer than themselves. This was the point at which the self-evident truth seemed to people to be that they were being dudded. And it is galling to have politicians deny what seems as plain as the nose on your face.

That the citizenry should lose faith in discourse is a high price for a nation to pay for this failure. Destructive post-truth paradoxes have included the recourse of people to wishful thinking in their search for truths they can believe. The demagogues see their moment—the people's disappointment at being misled causes them to prefer outright lies.

But the equivocal nature of truth shouldn't obscure the obvious. It is possible to demolish a lie, if you have evidence and vigilant courts. It is much harder to take the wishfulness out of a half-truth, especially if it talks about the future that offers itself to lazy thinking as "anyone's guess." People accept the scandalous fabrications of Trump's untruths—the "birther" slur, for example—precisely because they are scandalized by what they have been led to believe by more sober orators that has turned out to be so far from the truth.

Writing about totalitarian states in her epic study *Origins of Totalitarianism*, Hannah Arendt observed: "In an ever-changing, incomprehensible world the masses had reached the point where they would, at the same time, believe everything and nothing, think that everything was possible and nothing was true. . . . Mass propaganda discovered that its audience was ready at all times to believe the worst, no matter how absurd, and did not particularly object to being deceived because it held every statement to be a lie anyhow."

## post-truth

THE VERY PREFIX "post-" that makes post-truth such a scandal, can be seen to have been growing horns and a tail for the previous thirty years.

The Oxford dictionary pointed to an expansion in meaning of the prefix. "Rather than simply referring to the time after a specified situation or event—as in post-war or post-match"—it has taken on the meaning of "belonging to a time in which the specified concept has become unimportant or irrelevant." The nuance originates mid-twentieth century, they write, and has been used in various formations including post-national (1945), post-racial (1971) and post-feminist.

Some of this could be sheeted home to academic versions of European Marxist philosophies being garbled into tall tales of relativism. Post-structuralism was devised in scholarly circles to label a kind of social theory that described a conceptual move following from structuralism. That move highlighted the way that contrasts could be differently arranged in any array of terms and in so doing change the meaning. This theory emphasized perspective, but leading proponents were misread as relativist. Foucault and Derrida were especially the targets of Anglophone philosophers with their own views on common sense. This grew into an ill-informed McCarthyism that took a xenophobic approach to reading another tradition.

The post-structuralist philosophies in the original were not relativist but perspectivalist, aiming their challenge at the simple scientistic model of truth that had dominated empiricist traditions. Science itself had been re-evaluating the model at least since Heisenberg and quantum physics. But reported to the wider world from the academy in a garbled form, the assertion of relativism alarmed Conservatives because it erased the self-evidence of traditional meanings and particularly of social meanings. Historical social change was already overwhelming the old certainties; what the huge forces of industrializing had begun the impetus of globalization accelerated. Populism blamed the messenger.

But the post-prefix by itself was well designed for the populists' scandal. It became itself a signifier for change. This was even more evident in the notion of the post-modern, which came to stand in for post-structuralism although it was not in fact a synonym. In the popular discourse about the frightening pace of change, "post-modern" really captured something. The idea that we were already beyond the modern suggested we had already surpassed the present before we had properly arrived at it and this must mean that we were "getting ahead of ourselves." This disturbing temporality of the post- prefix generally fascinated the commentariat.

Post-truth has become the latest hysterical cry in the face of an implausible progression. Post-truth is an ingenious compression of many sleights of hand.

It has coalesced out of the imagined fear of the "future present," and of these foreign philosophies—Marxism, feminism, and identity politics—that were denying the apparently obvious.

Post-truth is a journalistic construct, and a good example of the rhetorical shift in political discourse amplified by social media and digital disruption. The associative slide from post-war to post-modern to post-truth loses referential directness until all it carries of the prefix is the connotation. No serious philosophy contends that there is no longer any such thing as truth. But the ineluctable complication of the notion in the face of the presence together in the public space of different languages and cultures has led to a re-think. Now, at the same time as observing the perspectival character of all statements, the new thinking affirms how styles of expression have greater, rather than less, probity than previously thought.

## fake news

"LEGACY" JOURNALISM, WITH its protocols of independent reporting of facts and authoritative comment or opinion has been overwhelmed by media of another order. As the populist turbulence of 2016 played out, it became clear that it was not just that print media has been eclipsed by cheaper online distribution.

It was the loss of authority of the traditional "editorial environment," previously so significant to the success of the leading mastheads in the days when they led opinion and advertising followed. Now as social media takes on more of the news dissemination, the tail is wagging the dog.

The concentration of press ownership, and the aggressive use that some proprietors have been prepared to make of it, had already reduced the prospects for an independent-minded journalism that might protect the fourth estate. Now the habits of social media change the value of free speech. Not only is mainstream media losing its revenue base to social media at a dizzying rate (in 2016, the operating profit of *The New York Times* fell by 13%, to $51.5 million while Facebook's net income tripled in the same period to $1.51 billion, as *The Guardian* editor Katharine Viner reported.) Social media is imposing, through its business model, a wholly different driver of influence. The "like" and the "click" is overtaking the traditional editorial curation of opinion-makers and even of media-owners in setting the agenda of news.

Despite the hope for the internet as a cultural commons, social media has disrupted practices of rights and democracy. The growth of the citizen journalist, the blog, and the YouTube video hasn't done much for freedom of the press. It seems the process has been hijacked by a concentrating of corporate interest greater than the feared traditional media ownership that cross-media rules have tried previously to offset.

Katharine Viner reports that a former specialist in high-traffic viral stories for *Gawker*, Neetzan Zimmerman, has said: "Nowadays it's not important if a story's real, the only thing that really matters is whether people click on it." The *modus operandi* of social media now defines the field: "If a person is not sharing a news story, it is, at its core, not news."

The tailored news feeds and feedback loops in chat rooms on social media sees a fragmenting of the public sphere in a way feared by defenders of free speech. The filter bubble is now dictating news. It crystallizes the antinomy between serving the market and retaining a free press as an organ of democracy. The importance of reportage uncovering unpleasant facts in an imperfect world becomes greater rather than less.

There is a difference between creating deceptive information to persuade people to vote otherwise than they would have ("I will bring back your coal mining jobs") and the political "puff" rhetoric that inclines toward a different kind of future—“make America great again”; “Take Back Control.” Beyond the filter bubble, the extremity of the like/click business model delivers fake news, stories designed purely to get attention and traffic onto websites by gaming the algorithms of the social media platforms.

The content of fake news may have been manufactured out of speculation, prejudice and wishful thinking (lying about what took place in Aleppo, covering up what took place in the hacking of Democratic servers or in the bedroom of a luxury Moscow hotel) and the cynicism of those who produce it is egregious. But lying is not new to the species. The fraud, the set-up, and deceit are all enduring threats to the public interest, as they have ever been. Before social media, deceit, and cover-up were still possible, perhaps even more possible. The promulgating of misinformation has been part and parcel of politics since the Trojan Horse.

What is new is the leveraging of a thousand tiny preferences into a tsunami of falsehood on social media.

## political correctness

WHEN IT OCCURS in law, as in the *Racial Vilification Act*, political correctness becomes a kind of bureaucratic action, which may explain why it is bracketed with other modern evils like "red tape" in the smear of "bureaucracy gone mad."

But "political correctness" as a charge against political discourse stands for more than labels and correct speech. The social ill that PC language addresses—bias against minorities and especially bias against sexuality, gender, and race expressed in ordinary language—presents speech as a kind of action and not as something distinct from it.

This view of language arises from post-structuralist and semiotic theories of language, picked up by the progressive side of politics as "identity politics." It focuses on the marginalizing of gender and race, rather than on class conflict. It has had, as one of its effects, the pitting of working class people against "others" that they are chided to make space for.

Some cite political correctness as a cause of Donald Trump's election win, saying that the apparent favoring of minorities in this concern angered those parts of the electorate who were feeling the pain of job losses in the "de-industrialized" rust-belt of the United States. And certainly, the loss of a world that the retreat of manufacturing has brought on, both there and in the North of England ahead of the Brexit vote, is a visceral cause of despair in those areas.

Although political correctness, then, has been aimed at enhancing or promoting equality, its directives are received as overruling a kind of class politics in favor of "others" who then receive preferential treatment. It is also experienced as a form of bureaucracy, appearing autocratic and as a challenge to individual freedoms, including free speech. Stalin is mentioned; Orwellian "double speak" is invoked. Inclusive language gets on the one hand lumped in with other bureaucratic measures like positive discrimination that become pejoratively described as "social engineering." On the other, its artificiality groups it with political spin and types of public speech that have a quite different intent, a consciousness of language that is heard as "weasel words," and which may smell of propaganda, cover-up and fraud.

These unfortunate tendencies have driven anger against social inclusion, and characterized political correctness as somehow in conflict with liberal freedoms, especially free speech, with its wholly different concept of what speech is to the democratic process.

Politically correct language may or may not have worked to repress robust discussion around immigration policy in the Western democracies now feeling a populist backlash. But on the ground, political correctness has collided with the consequences of free trade and increased immigration. The higher visibility of people from minority ethnicities in workplaces, or of women in positions of authority and LGBT couples celebrating their unions has been conflated into a resentment against political correctness. There are several different policy landscapes behind this increased visibility, but they are lumped together in an effect that recently has been perceived by some not to benefit them. And yet political correctness is felt to shame anyone complaining about these changes.

Take Brexit as a case in point: the surprising referendum result seemed to build not on economic arguments about membership of the European Union, but sentiments about a loss of precedence for old-style Anglo male majorities in a world ruled by edicts from elsewhere. There was undeniably a degree of xenophobia in this sentiment, which was fueled by the rhetoric of the "leave" campaign. And while the "destiny of a sovereign nation" was invoked as pretext, the referendum to decide on whether Britain should leave the European Union was held largely for party-political purposes to outflank the radical right of the Tory party for the group of moderates trying to keep control of it.

The move spectacularly backfired when it collided with the agitprop of a populist mood that sold a kind of magical thinking to a disenchanted constituency—the pilloried "sunlit uplands with unicorns." And in the wake of the vote, the struggle within major parties—and particularly the governing party of Conservatives who had by that point lost their majority in the Commons—was more and more nakedly about what would protect their political interest rather than any view of the public good.

It could be seen from a country mile that "no-deal" Brexit was likely to vandalize the economy, and hurt worst those who had been most susceptible to the "leave" pitch about taking back control from politically correct elites—the working people and retirees who had suffered under austerity mandated by the fallout of the Global Financial Crisis. And yet, no figure emerged from the right or the left that could take the situation out of the paralysis of a parliamentary democracy stymied by the consequences of the populism it had stirred up.

At bottom, the resentment was justified, perhaps, in protesting an unequal distribution of wealth; it only misidentified the culprits as the minorities who were championed by the political correctness of a certain kind of speech.

The prospect of the political sphere as in any way open to the future—or even to those people already born but not yet of voting age—became obscured in the xenophobic mood. If democratic representatives genuinely thought ahead, to the world of strangers to come and with what we should wish to welcome them, the short-sightedness of this politics would be clear. There would be a view from which this myopia is bordering on corrupt. Sadly, that vista looks destined to be seen in the 20/20 of hindsight.

## why free speech

THE POST-TRUTH phenomenon, the advent of fake news, and the opprobrium of political correctness is more disturbing because of the scale on which it could attack the credibility of politics and the public discourse that supports it.

The guarantee of free speech is made in liberal democracies across the "free world." At common law, there has long been a "negative" right to freedom of speech, constraining others from obstructing it. In Europe, free speech is explicitly guaranteed by the European Convention on Human Rights, ratified by all member states. It was taken into British Law by the 1998 *Human Rights Act*, Article 10, which provides the right to freedom of expression subject to certain restrictions that are "in accordance with law" and "necessary in a democratic society."

In the United States, free speech is famously guaranteed in the Constitution by the First Amendment, adopted in 1791: "Congress shall make no law respecting an establishment of religion, or prohibiting the free exercise thereof; or abridging the freedom of speech, or of the press; or the right of the people peaceably to assemble, and to petition the Government for a redress of grievances."

The first amendment begins with the guarantee of religious freedom because it is at the hands of religious authorities that settlers originally felt the coercion of authority on ideas and their expression. It sets the context for free speech as one in which truth and belief are close cousins. The Europe of the eighteenth century emerged from medieval practices of "revelation" of truth, including torture, toward a conviction that there was an impartial truth that could be recognized by reasonable people as evidence-based and true for any observer. The conviction went hand-in-hand with enlightenment values in Newtonian physics and the experimental method of the physical sciences. In parallel, the political consensus to be found in a democracy was thought to emerge from the ability to express ideas and to discuss them with each other—the right of association was similarly regarded as essential to the democratic process.

"Those who won our independence . . . believed that freedom to think as you will and to speak as you think are means indispensable to the discovery and spread of political truth" as Justice Brandeis eloquently put it, dissenting, in *Whitney v. California* [1927].

Attempts by authority to constrain this freedom, by restricting what could be said when and to whom, were regarded with suspicion; the right has been jealously guarded. As the singular way to establish truth in the political community, the defending of free speech grew in importance, and jurists of the early twentieth century expanded the application of the first amendment in the United States, extending it to more situations than it had been held to affect in the nineteenth.

The virtue in having "the freedom to think as you will and to speak as you think" lies in the potency of ideas shared for the viability of a political community. The seriousness of this imagined forum was underpinned by an assumption of sincerity, of a close bond held between truth and belief. Is it this bond that has come loose?

The perfect democrat was a philosopher and a lover of truth, but as the politics of enlightenment has matured and aged, this Platonism shows signs of wear. Actually, twentieth-century political history shows that people believe a thing for many reasons other than its truth—because they want to believe it's true, because it looks familiar to them, because it seems likely or plausible, because it is said by someone they know and/or trust. Philosophy is replete with warnings against "invalid reasoning."

And then there are the less respectable reasons—because something is amazing, unlikely, sensational or scandalous. Because it offers an easy answer, or a way not to answer, a quick fix, a pretext or an alibi. Because it makes things previously believed more likely. Because it is too frightening to entertain the alternative. And so on.

The point of the forum of free speech is that it's meant to measure plausibility, and average out the reasoning. It proceeds on the principle that "you can't fool all of the people all of the time." But in the closed forums of social media perhaps you can.

"Sticks and stones may break my bones but words will never hurt me." Distinguishing speech from action, as the liberal traditions do, tends to an oversimplification. It overlooks the existence of kinds of speech that are held even in the notion of free speech to be actively dangerous, or leading to special harm. For example, it is actionable at law to sue where one is defamed, because what is said about a person matters to their reputation, and indeed forms it. It has been illegal in wartime to discuss certain information widely—"loose talk costs lives."

The UK *Human Rights Act* lists kinds of speech which may be circumscribed on the grounds that it may be damaging; the right includes the freedom to hold opinions, and to receive and impart information and ideas, but provides a long list of restrictions to protect interests of national security, territorial integrity or public safety, prevention of disorder or crime, protection of health or morals, protection of the reputation or the rights of others, preventing the disclosure of information received in confidence and maintaining the authority and impartiality of the judiciary.

Law itself is a powerful counter-argument to the liberal assumption that speech is opposed to action; both legislation and the opinions of judges are potent forms of speech that become a kind of action. It follows that some speech can cause harm, and that political correctness despite the opprobrium addresses a real issue for the democratic polis.

## propaganda

NONE OF THE provisions of the US *Human Rights Act*, much less of the American constitution, foresee a world in which the value of free speech is being undermined by discounting the value placed on the truth of it, or challenging the self-evidence of this in public life.

Of course, as they famously say, "in war the first casualty is truth." But here, the threat to free speech is imagined to come from an authoritarian repression of it. It is not anticipated in the law and practice defending free speech that it would be encroached on by the trivializing of it.

Propaganda was the new weapon of authoritarian states in the twentieth century. But the democratic nations of Europe, the Commonwealth, and the United States, accepting their radical distinction as countries of "the Free World," were perhaps blind to threats to free expression that might come from another direction.

The excising from the ambit of "freedom of speech" of statements "done for the purpose of making a profit" was compromised by the back door in the Supreme Court decision that allowed political donations by corporations to be regarded as a form of free speech (*Citizens United v. Federal Election Commission* 2010). In a regressive line of thought, and using the fiction of corporate personhood, it was held that paying a representative to speak for you is a democratic right that companies as well as individuals can claim. The result has been an increase in lobbyists, special pleading and rent-seeking that influences the conduct of democratic processes under the protection of "freedom of speech."

Not all expression was traditionally accorded the status of free speech protected by the first amendment. A class of representations made in public places and addressing the populace was not regarded as political at all. The provisions that exempted "commercial speech" from the operation of the first amendment are perhaps now worth a second look. Those provisions provide that if an expression is "speech done on behalf of a company or individual for the purpose of making a profit" then it is not protected in the same way.

This "commercial speech" has not been recognized as presenting a danger to political speech. And yet, it is precisely speech made for purpose of making a profit that has evolved to inject rhetoric into the political discourse at the expense of impartial truth and, further, to create the circumstances in which propaganda can rival it. What else is fake news?

The blindsiding of democratic discourse came from the conviction that motivated speech was the opposite of impartial speech, and that propaganda would be forced on a people only by autocratic authority. But we see that a culture of marketing, with its manipulations of affect and its appeal to wishfulness, propagated in a landscape of social media, might compel assent from the populace like the fear of authority did in the totalitarian state.

Since the Supreme Court decision of *Buckley versus Valeo* (1976), money talks. Several further cases of the court have extended the protection of the first amendment to campaign funding by corporations and wealthy individuals.

We don't perhaps see the political import of marketing or "commercial speech" because we don't appreciate that truth in the guise of information has become a marketable commodity, and how power takes effect sometimes through truth. Yet this paradox has flourished in the "post-truth" and "fake news" intrusions into recent political discourse. Now we need to look at the drama occurring off-camera.

It works for the "alt-right" that relativism should prevail, although they bitterly denounce it—if truth is relative, then reality can be left to happen as inequality, and even fraud, go unchecked. By reality is actually meant "economic reality" which, in the context of this "post"-moment, is the only grounding of a truth, the only thing that emerges as credible; "it's the economy, stupid," "the bottom line."

The loss of probity in language does not prevent the structures of value from operating in favor of the "real world" of economics. The beneficiary of this slide into relativism remains the flow of global capital that continues to make money whatever happens.

Power is being stolen from out of the public sphere in this evacuation of meaning, siphoned off into the value-creation of the economic which emerges more and more as the only solid indicator of reality that is trusted. Facing this prospect will call for a changed understanding of the power of language and the defense of free speech.

AS A FOUNDING value in the liberal thought systems of the West, free speech is enshrined in constitutional documents throughout the democratic world. Ideas of fake news, post-truth and political correctness come out in resistance against the values of free speech with their strong political pedigree.

Often run together, the phenomena of fake news and post-truth have differing provenance—while fake news plays off the idea of a free press, held to be critical to the functioning of a democracy, post-truth is a diagnosis of a discursive disorder that has been developing since the period "post-war," most especially in the figure of the politically correct. This is all seen to challenge the democratic when it takes place as a contest between political and commercial speech.

*[five]*

# *[free world]*

THE BERLIN WALL, for so long during the Cold War a sinister icon of totalitarianism defended by sniper shot, is once again the focus of protest. Only this time, instead of calling for it to be pulled down in a brave and deadly confrontation, the call is to leave it standing. Or at least, that part of it that contains the memorial to aspirations of the free world, the "East Side Gallery."

The contest between communism and capitalism is so last century. Now the protestors clash with real estate developers who want to pull down the wall to make way for an access road to luxury flats.

In the wake of World War II, it was briefly imagined that good had triumphed over evil and delivered freedom from political oppression. The free world became understood as freedom from domination by authoritarian governments.

But the notion of the free world was riddled with ironies from the start because Stalin, who as leader of Russia had led arguably the most effective campaign against Hitler and the Axis powers, rapidly became as totalitarian as the Nazi state. The Allies, who owed their victory in large part to Stalin, nevertheless quickly expelled the idea of Soviet Russia from the term. Most of what offended against the "free world" became concentrated as an attack on the ideology of communism, not fascism; despite having been the central Nazi threat, fascism rapidly retreated as a major foe. The free world, although self-styled defender of democracy, in effect defended capitalism.

Long after the end of the Cold War, with the rising popularity of far-right parties on the contemporary Western political landscape, German leader Angela Merkel was dubbed in the press the "Chancellor of the Free World" when chosen as *Time*'s 2015 Person of the Year. Although literally making a nonsense of the term, this recognized Germany's remarkable reinvention as a democratic state. It seems the idea of the free world had already descended into irrelevance at best, and satire at worst, when Donald Trump breathed new life into its absurdity.

Now commentators have wondered in print whether "the West might be nearing the end of its shelf life," and suggesting that "under President Trump, we cannot assume that America is still the leader of the free world" (*The Atlantic*, January 24, 2017). The shifting ironies and ambivalences identify the phrase as an American fantasy, justifying its world prominence and "exceptionalism" that, seen from other perspectives like the modern configuration of the European Union and the Chinese "Belt and Road" push, may be losing plausibility.

The election of a reality TV president was greeted with black jokes about "We Shall Overcomb." There was something about Trump that suggested the "Ken" doll of an American dream in which anyone can grow up to be president. The post-truth hallmark, the divorce of reality from discourse, characterized the Trump 2016 and 2020 election campaigns. It was about everything and nothing. And even, when speaking as the President, it became increasingly difficult to say which of his contradictory statements he meant, and whether it would be better or worse for the country if he "walked back" what he has said on any given occasion. The news was full of Trump outrages, but no one was watching the structural stuff—the theft of democracy by a corrupted political *mise-en-scène*.

In an impressive essay, "Enemy Within: American Politics in the Time of Trump," Don Watson moves through the landscape of middle America in the election year 2016. His observation could leave us pessimistic in the wake of the election. Even though it was written before the race was won, it provides a clear-sighted view of why, whether Hilary Clinton or Donald Trump won, the case for American exceptionalism was lost.

Watson defines Trump as a fascist of sorts but argues that two centuries of democracy make America less vulnerable than Weimar Germany. The American Constitution, as experts remind us, was stress-tested in the Civil War. And maybe Trump doesn't care enough to dismantle it. He's been heard to complain that "being president is harder work than I thought."

## the end of something

THE BACKSTORY TO the "free world" came from a political history of revolutions that set nations up as liberal democracies with free enterprise as the economic motor. Liberalism and capitalism grew together in societies envisaged as promoting political individualism and private wealth.

As these political "bourgeois" revolutions were given shape by parallel industrial revolutions, the contrast between ruling class and masses kept its expression as a distinction primarily in wealth. The working people emerged as subjected not to the King but to the Capitalist; whoever owned the means of production (as Marx famously diagnosed it) had the means to generate wealth that belonged properly to all.

Marx's analysis is well known—the working people had become wage slaves and their lot, as he saw it in Victorian Britain, was no better (and perhaps worse) than when they had toiled on the land for the aristocrat's enrichment. What was needed, for the people to be truly liberated, was a workers' revolution. Marxism was from the outset a rival account to liberalism of the perfect economic arrangement in an industrial age.

But the end of the Cold War made it briefly seem as though democratic capitalism had won. The end of the Cold War gave rise to a new free world discourse. The accomplishment of the capitalist mode of production was declared yet the tone of discussions that announced the "end of communism" and the "end of history" was apocalyptic. Derrida argues this totalizing—of the global no less than of the end—is an intellectual fault.

In *Specters of Marx*, he argues there could be no such thing as The End. The apocalypse is a biblical narrative and, while a story is entitled (even obliged) to end, the world and humankind and life in short is not a story. It won't end as such, even if it ceases, the planet made uninhabitable by environmental damage or climate change; or nations destroyed by nuclear war; or the human species overborne by artificial intelligence, or wiped out by pandemics of drug-resistant superbugs; or any of the other prognostication more or less credible being made on any day by doomsayers.

Derrida examined the ambivalent legacy of Marxism in new world order/s. He explored the hunch that history does not end, but would return as a specter, to haunt in new and different terms. Derrida credits Marx with sometimes seeing this, himself—that the end of history is, like the withering of the State, a fetishistic logic.

He argues that "production," "labour," and "capitalisation" as concepts will all exceed their shelf life as played out in the capitalist mode of production. The uncanny nature of technology—its production of virtual presence by making the not-quite-present and simulacral in teletechnology—is alarming in itself and subverts the essence of any ontology, haunting its hubris. In consequence, those neo-liberals who have celebrated the death of Marxism have spoken too soon—the glorious positivity to which they refer is itself haunted by those things it has not/not yet produced.

For example, perfect equality which is on its way, its lack merely empirical. Derrida is scathing about this political naivety, which he argues is a kind of cruelty, particular targeting Fukuyama and *The End of History and the Last Man*—to which we might add the trickle-down economics that we are presently promised will complete the economic miracle.

Democracy and freedom are traditionally the antidote of totalitarian methods. It is the pluralism of American political thinking that is meant to inoculate it. But capitalism gnaws at democracy from within. This scene Don Watson sets in a series of disturbingly lucid sketches. Perhaps the most eloquent is the final portrait of the airport hotel, "my own dark dogbox in the bar-less, café-less Holiday Inn."

> What were they thinking when they built that Holiday Inn? From what concept of humanity, what manner of philosophy, what thousand-year tradition of hospitality did it derive? . . . the answer is from no philosophy; no thought at all, except the thought of profit. (2016, 68)

## democracy as marketing

SOCIAL MEDIA, CLIMATE change, and terrorism have superseded the ideological rivalries of the Cold War, rendering them quaint. The free world now goes global—everyone tamed and brought to the table by avarice, the money to be made from trade.

The relentless pressure of the market is brought to bear around us in images everywhere—on phones, billboards, screens, and pages—nudging us toward an aesthetic that wants something from us. Marketing exerts its pressure in the representation itself, which is designed to make the viewer do something in response (buy the product/want the look/like the sentiment/vote for it).

Since Edward Bernays wrote *Crystallizing Public Opinion* in 1923, marketing has been the quiet force that has shaped culture in the West and remade it in its image. As he wrote (elsewhere): "The conscious and intelligent manipulation of the organized habits and opinions of the masses is an important element in democratic society." But Andy Warhol saw the companionship of democracy and marketing as less of a collusion: "You can be watching TV and see Coca-Cola, and you know that the President drinks Coca-Cola, Liz Taylor drinks Coca-Cola, and just think, you can drink Coca-Cola, too. A Coke is a Coke and no amount of money can get you a better Coke than the one the bum on the corner is drinking" (1975, 100–1).

There is something telling in the way there has become no opposition between these things, democracy and marketing; a seamlessness "between tickle and prickle," between cajoling and manipulating; between marketing Coke and selling politics. Between political speech and propaganda; the threat emerges now of an "enemy within" from marketing, spin, massaging the event into post-truth fake news. It culminates with the election of a reality TV president who is the classic simulacrum of a strong leader.

Baudrillard, who has done more than most theorists to inflate with hyperbole the virtual future, describes a political discourse that has lost touch with reality and now explodes in an echo-chamber of images without originals, of signs without real referents, in what he calls the "hyperreal." Baudrillard's dystopic view has been amplified since he wrote, by the advent of social media which seems to corroborate his theory post facto, and play out the kind of relativism he diagnoses.

Baudrillard remarks in *Simulacra and Simulation* on Nixon as a puppet; well before Trump For President, Baudrillard raised the likely prospect of the U.S. president being nothing more than a "mannequin of power"—and within the first 100 days of Trump's administration the specter of Watergate became stronger. Trump appeared as a puppet of forces he didn't understand, didn't respect or maybe didn't suspect. He appeared as the chat bot of the alt right, programmed to make like a "real person," on Twitter and on TV, to produce responses that please an audience, but without authenticity.

Through his first term, Trump has been a test of democracy, a chance to find out whether the leader of the free world is now a purely ceremonial position. Trump tests democracy as marketing, a demonstration of whether voters will go with the virtual world and the inauthentic system—whether you could know it was a chat bot and vote for it anyway because it tells you what you want to hear.

Baudrillard observes the image eliminating its referent in the morphing of the free world into the cybersphere. Allowing for his rhetorical extravagance, it seems that by the "real" he means politics, and the scandal was not Watergate, or a simulation of it, but capital; "its instantaneous cruelty; its incomprehensible ferocity; its fundamental immorality — these are what are scandalous, unaccountable for in that system of moral and economic equivalence which remains the axiom of leftist thought, from Enlightenment theory to communism" (1994, 173).

## Stockholm syndrome

LONDON'S "BLACKBERRY RIOTS" in 2011 puzzled many traditional pundits accustomed to seeing mass riots as a prelude to protest about "rational" things like workers' pay and conditions. Instead, organizing via mobile phones, the rioters focused on looting stuff—High Street desirables like trainers and electronics.

The market is the "real," grinding its straw into gold beyond the reach of political representation. Political protest is dissipated in the narcotic of consumer desire. Or is desire for stuff the new political demand? Is the democratic urge now (following Warhol) about assuming the image with Nikes and iPhone? Representation in its double sense, the democratic notion and the image itself, are conflating in the hyperreal and warping the political. Baudrillard floats the possibility that capitalism is the source of this value relativism, causing the collapse of meaning in its instrumental reason that processes everything into the equivalence of exchange. The market is a phantom, a ghost in a machine for generating social worlds by endlessly creating and redistributing value as wealth.

In this, liberal democracy has become capital's free world partner. Or has democracy become co-opted by capital, moving from an obliging companion to a hostage to its fortune? American democracy is showing symptoms of Stockholm syndrome. It has been thought to be proof against this kind of ideological reification because of its pluralism. The plurality comes from each individual exercising their difference in the election of their representative. But this disguises the capture of democracy by capital; the buying of the election with political funding that threatens to bring the whole project undone.

As Wolfgang Streeck analyses it, in "How Will Capitalism End?":

> Capitalism and democracy had long been considered adversaries, until the post-war settlement seemed to have accomplished their reconciliation. Well into the twentieth century, owners of capital had been afraid of democratic majorities abolishing private property, while workers and their organizations expected capitalists to finance a return to authoritarian rule in defence of their privileges. Only in the Cold War world did capitalism and democracy seem to become aligned with one another, as economic progress made it possible for working-class majorities to accept a free-market, private-property regime, in turn making it appear that democratic freedom was inseparable from, and indeed depended on, the freedom of markets and profit-making. Today, however, doubts about the compatibility of a capitalist economy with a democratic polity have powerfully returned. (2014, 40)

The alleged covert action of manipulation through social media, fake news and wholesale hacking amplifies the libertarian tendency of the right and raises the specter: Can the democratic ideal survive these distortions? American democracy in its present form is seriously selective; disenfranchising many of the poor and ghettoed through voluntary voting. By its actions as a world power, both its commercial and military, the American sphere of influence disenfranchises many more in satellite states who can never register to vote.

The primary support Trump has is reportedly among white working-class men. Are they ignorant of their self-interest—how can a millionaire who profits from the present system be expected to change it? Do they ask themselves how the leader of a single nation, even one as powerful as the United States, could overcome the processes of globalization? How can anyone turn back the clock to a time when America was Great?

Or is it that they feel their self-interest in another register? The psychology of voting, as a self-assertion, may be satisfied by resonating with the candidate's foul mouth, his lack of political correctness, or his belligerence. This version of democracy is closer to the totalitarian sirens' song. In this version, the voter is absorbed into the ideology and resists any argument to the contrary with outbursts of feeling that range from dismissive to violent. This is tribal democracy, magical thinking, elements of which are embodied in the two-party systems of many modern nations.

Trump's rhetoric frequently uses intimidation to carry ideology into the political discourse. The bluster, the insults, the demagoguery, the adjuring to violence (suggesting someone could shoot the candidate opposing the second amendment), the normalizing of extremism (quoting the Ku Klux Klan), the demonizing of the opposition ("crooked Hillary," "lock her up")—these are all tactics of an affective register that nod toward terror.

Support for Trump is growing on the fertile ground that marketing and spin have prepared. These compromise the realistic prospect of free choice in a world of disinformation and the covert influence of political funding. It's the preparation for democracy as a tribal event, and for a general election as theatrical spectacle staged against a background of powerlessness and cynicism that has rendered the pluralism of representative democracy almost inert.]

## who broke the business model?

FREE SPEECH, FREE press, free expression: previously relishing their free status, these cultural artifacts now experience an uncertain future, as the commodity fetishism of "free stuff" captures global cultural markets.

An unholy confluence of events has led to a developing global ecology in which some cultural forms are not just starved, but may face extinction. The reason is the dramatic change the internet has wrought in the means of financial support for them. The cultural industries of publishing, design and journalism face a global crisis commonly attributed to the growth of the internet. These are three important sources of culture production, and their individual producers have perhaps never found it easy to make a living doing it. But it's notable that there seems at present to be a threat to these products that are of an existential order.

The movement of content online has been building, and is now described as having crested and broken "like a tsunami" on traditional methods of cultural consumption, inundating them and making them all but unviable in their present modes. Print journalism, already challenged by the move to video news, has lost much of its customary advertising revenue to websites that target the consumer without the need for an editorial setting. Meanwhile, building an online print journalism that pays has been hampered by the expectation that web content is free.

The deeper threat to journalism in the move to the internet is said to be the fragmentation of the public sphere. Whereas in the past, we would all read the same front page, establishing the daily news as a public discourse, today Google will tailor a search to the searches previously made by the user, producing a different set of outcomes for a researcher in cultural studies than for a real estate investor. The production of a "reality stream" that does not contradict your point of view has been cited as a factor in the 2016 U.S. presidential election.

Publishing has its own version of the internet raiders breaking the business model. It is called Amazon. The online retailers of books have been able to offer lower prices to consumers worldwide by mass discounting using market power. Online retailers' global discounting has gutted the gentlemen's agreement known as the "territories" arrangements which supported the Berne Convention.

Publishers fear now that only block-busters and best-sellers have the revenue potential to survive in an increasingly monopoly-driven market. Among other casualties, literary fiction and nonfiction, regional literatures, and other niche publishing are threatened with unviability because they cannot match the scale of this global movement of merchandise online. Meanwhile, the emergence of e-book publishing as a more cost-effective alternative has not yet been able to attract critical recognition.

The internet as cause and effect of globalization is now entrenched in the market: its speed, automation, and reach contributed significantly to the panic of the Global Financial Crisis. Seen against this background, the prospects for cultural products and their consumption seem dependent on markets at odds with their "free" ethos.

So free stuff becomes an ambivalent cultural value. Writers want to be free to write, while readers want freely to read. But who, then, will pay for the labor of making culture? Is it inevitable that free speech must be indentured to advertising and marketing, which is the traditional business model, in order to pay its way? Must literature "meet the market" in order to be read? To attempt an answer means bringing the free market into focus, and examining the political economy underpinning cultural labor and products.

One bastion of free stuff was previously found in the ideas of academic and creative freedom that underpinned humanities research and artistic endeavor. But as public funding for the arts is pulled back, and private patronage in the form of sales and sponsorship takes its place, it brings with it an ideological assertion that challenges the "free" values previously cherished in these institutions. Perhaps as a way of deflecting blame for cutting funding, it has come to be said that these pursuits should be "paying their way." The values of "art for art's sake" and "free thought" are deeply entrenched in ways of understanding cultural production and so this challenge inaugurates a large cultural shift.

It has made of the artist an entrepreneur, and the university a corporate enterprise. With education reconceived as an export sector, the continuing economic rationalizing of universities ties academic activities like teaching and research to instrumental priorities that do not fund cultural and intellectual life for their own sake. The ideological intent of what is presented as economic reform is seen in, among other changes, the encroachment on working conditions of academics—the abolition of tenure, and the outlawing of negative public comment by academics on university policy and conduct. The universities defend these measures as providing flexibility in employment and protecting their brands. But does intellectual freedom drag down the bottom line? Far from enhancing the product and brand, intellectual freedom is now seen as an impediment and an impost on the university, which suggests the target is something other than the education budget.

Each of these challenges—to the press, to literature and to academic freedom—in different ways exemplify the expansion of instrumental thinking into cultural pursuits that were previously free from it. The lingua franca of this crisis has become the "breaking of the business model."

The internet challenge has been: How to get free stuff to pay? "To monetise" is the new verb for it. The business model for e-commerce monetizes in exemplary fashion. It no longer needs to provide anything other than the classified ad display. The typical advertisement now appearing on realestate .com would have previously appeared in the newspaper with its high costs of printing and distribution, not to mention the exorbitant cost of maintaining an editorial environment of news reporting and quality journalism around it.

Wikipedia defines a business model as "the rationale of how an organisation creates, delivers and captures value (economic, social, cultural . . . )." Familiar business models include the flat pack DIY home furnishing (Ikea), bricks-and-clicks (department stores online), bait-and-hook (printer and cartridges), franchise (Muffin Break), and online auction (eBay).

The idea of the business model as "rationale" calls up the skewed logic of instrumental thinking. The capture of culture by the business model, and its apparent loss of value, is a hostage-taking of global proportion.

## from the masses to the mob

IN FACEBOOK, THE marketing technology which begins in the early twentieth century with Bernays finds its fullest expression. Now not only is "Like" the driver of economic means, but it also takes over the political space. Democracy is appropriated as "I Like."

The blindsiding of democratic discourse has come from the free world assumption that propaganda would be forced on a people only by autocratic authority. But now in social media we see that marketing, with its manipulations of affect and its appeal to wishfulness, can compel assent from the populace.

Hannah Arendt, who escaped German totalitarianism for the haven of American democracy, coined the phrase "the banality of evil" for the terrifying advent of "no thought at all." She was reporting on the trial of the Nazi Eichmann in the *New York Times*.

Arendt argues totalitarianism is possible only once technology has produced a world of surplus, including surplus humanity configured as the masses. The totalitarian order may be masked at first by the tyranny or violence required to set it up. But totalitarianism is linked essentially to technological thinking, premised on the subordination of all as means to any end whatever. Totalitarianism and technology are species of the same instrumental reasoning. Totalitarianism, through the instrument of terror, establishes motion as the only principle of government. Terror eliminates all individuation, action, and conviction, creating the population as a mass bound so closely together as to stand for one thing only (the state as fatherland, historical destiny or whatever).

Freedom cannot literally be erased from the souls of humans, Arendt points out, because it springs from every new birth as a beginning again of the world. Extinguishing that freedom happens not by murder and genocide (although these are demonstrations of the principle of terror), but through terror convincing the people to surrender freedom as an unnecessary and dangerous superfluity, and to accept that the individual is only an instrument for the movement of history or destiny through the population. Terror trains its subjects in an indifference to their fates, so that they can be executioner at one time and victim at another without questioning, she argues.

But to do this requires a perversion of the human condition itself, which is as a thinking acting being. It requires an agent as toxic as terror to drive the human personality to partition off this essence of itself. Terror can convince the people to place self-survival above the human.

Arendt traces the intellectual possibility of totalitarianism, and its novelty in human government, to the Idealist thought-systems of the nineteenth century—Kant, Hegel, Marx, Darwin. Although obviously a perversion, nevertheless the sublation of the particular moment into a stage in a progression toward the expression of an ideal, be it History, Nation, or Nature, allows for the particular to be wholly consumed in its relation to the whole.

This is logic set over against reality, she argues; this is the logic of the idea defeating the vivacity of particular events and sensations. It produces ideologies, which are literally ideas taken as logics insulated by their conceptual movement from any empirical particulars that might challenge them at individual moments.

Facebook is on its way to world domination, and this is not really hyperbole. It has now harnessed political desires to the commercial and consumer desires originally monetized; it is now in principle a virtual state without constitution or border limit, except this machine running on the compulsory desires (rather than fears) of its subjects.

Facebook's 1.6 billion users are all being swayed to Like what they see the world over. That's at the level of content. Facebook is only sixteen years old and it is already a rival political platform to that of some nation states—consider its role in events such as the Arab spring. But Facebook mobilizes desire far more profoundly for its own profit. The algorithms capturing data and directing it to the advertisers' message are the unseen spies that manipulate the Facebook "community" to express their preferences so that Facebook can monetize them. The algorithms mine our likes and dislikes for a marketing fortune as we track across social networks in search of meaningful connection.

When this underbelly is revealed, Facebook appears monstrous. It is above democratic safeguards, outside institutions protecting its participants from manipulation, predation and coercion—worse, its business model is specifically designed to prey on the feelings and tastes of users and, unbeknown to them, drive them toward what will make Facebook more money. Simple goal: keep people on screen as long as possible to give maximum exposure to the advertisers' message. But also, maximize the extraction of their desires and fears as metadata, the better to exploit these on an ongoing basis.

Since these algorithms are embedded in the technology of the internet, through Facebook and Google in particular, you can no longer participate in the social world without making this perpetual donation of time and emotion. These multinational corporations reserve the power not to pay tax to terrestrial governments, moving their putative earnings to lower-tax "environments" offshore while they threaten nation states with moving their physical operations, too, to cheaper jurisdictions (with the loss to jobs and local economies that this implies).

Has instrumental reason captured democracy completely in the advent of the internet? There is no expression made on Facebook, however altruistic, that isn't potentially exploited for marketing purposes; no artless preference not monetized and no social bond not coopted to someone's profit. In effect we are already being taxed by this virtual state of Facebook/Amazon/Google, our tithe extracted every time we perform any online action—and every subject is obliged to perform basic actions online now, everything from banking to applying for dog licenses and visas. Google takes its cut; Facebook is paid in "big data."

Marketing may be built into democracy, since democracy must win individual voter support. But the constant recording of the "will of the majority," in trivialities like Twitter trending, Facebook likes, and app store picks, gives democracy a different feel. Less agora, more coliseum. Suddenly, crossed with marketing, the preferences of the majority become overwhelming, even menacing. Facebook and its rivals are hoovering up the will of the people for unparalleled profit, permitting the slide of democracy into the open jaws of the market.

It raises the final free world irony; that capital, too, might present an ideology on the Arendt definition. Through the notion of "free" that lies behind its democratic guises, the freedom of will, thought, expression, and choice are boiled down to a common fulcrum of desire that now moves the political-economic firmament.

THE NARRATIVE OF the Cold War was perceived with the breaking up of the Eastern bloc as one of "How the West was won." But commentators underestimated history. Instead of withering away, totalitarianism "flipped" into a global movement of capital dedicated to nothing more than its own momentum.

We should be re-reading Arendt on the totalitarian ideology and Baudrillard on the rise of the simulacral. But this is complicated by the decline in prestige of knowledge from an increasingly marginalized humanities, and an increasing commodification of text in publishing and journalism.

Facebook proves to be the exemplar of it, a morphing of the democratic into mass marketing and the curdling of the hope of freedom in the globalizing of it.

*technological thinking*

*[six]*

# *[free choice]*

WHEN I STAND before the dairy cabinet in the supermarket, I see it has arranged in it any number of different kinds of the same thing.

The display presents an overwhelming seeming-variety—low fat, full-fat, flavored, and fruit added—that masks the fact that "it's all yoghurt." I am attempting to choose well, as the cooking shows and dietary columns adjure. But the shelves of nearly identical products call up the challenge of how in general I make my choice.

While our free choice is held out as a leading democratic virtue, the reasons behind our choices are rarely as rational or self-aware as they appear. We make choices in order to be the kind of person we are urged to become as much as we make our choices as pre-existing rational beings. More, we make ourselves as social beings through our choices. These are based not just on what we need or what we want. Choice often becomes about how we see ourselves in relation to others—are we poorer, posher, traditional, sensible, more chic, more savvy?

Take the example of "good choices." These are epitomized in the healthy food choices we are urged to make by public health campaigns acting on obesity, heart disease, and other ailments. Through the idea of making good choices, self-actualizing through choice slips easily into the demand to conform. Literally, the ingestion of the norm; the good choice is applauded as one that tends toward health which is held to be a self-evident good. While some kinds of food and drink are better for the body than others, in becoming the public health discourse of "good choices" a great deal more is added to the choice than a reasonable observation on what promotes well-being.

The language of good choices comes out of a public health discourse that has more than the consumer's best interest at heart. It's the impact on the social body that is largely behind the public health push—not least because sick populations cost money in lost productivity and medical resources. The rhetoric of the "good choice" assumes that I can choose my state of health and well-being, and contrasts with the "poor choice" which makes ill health the individual's responsibility.

The shadow behind choice is the operation of addiction—sugar, tobacco, alcohol—which is by definition "not a choice." Addiction compels, which is why Coca-Cola *et al.* solicit it. The public health discourse seeks to make the individual responsible for shortcomings in the economic scene that allows producers to make money from food and products that make people sick. The idea that the consumer rather than capital ought to be adjusted lies behind the rhetoric of the "good" choice. There is a level of injustice in the notion of a good choice or a poor one being the consumer's sole responsibility.

The occurrence of "self-destructive behaviors," from overeating to smoking and alcohol, are also demonstrably linked to rates of poverty and access to alternatives, while the huge profits made by the wholesale marketing of fast food and beverages—manufacturers who sweeten the pill quite literally to bind the consumer to the product—are largely absent from view in the public health campaigns.

Paradoxically, while the public health campaign works against the marketing of specific food and beverage products, it works with the same material; the art of persuasion that is aimed at our identity. Based as it apparently is on what we as consumers want, marketing—the science of persuasion—ought to be the opposite of state authority. The action of the market and the power of the choice of the people could be thought the antithesis of state-centralized coercion.

Yet marketing has significant political force. It belongs to democracy, as the kind of power that is based on what people want. But it is also a threat to it, persuading people to do things not for their self-interest but through a scaled-up peer pressure that is more about feelings (of inclusion, self-image, and identity among others).

Marketing plays its part in "managing populations." But marketing exercises its pressure differently from governmental power. Marketing urges norms, and it functions through powerful mechanisms of social recognition. This play on the prompting of people's desire for recognition is underestimated in the shape of contemporary democracy. It is efficient, as the market is said to be—why force people to be what the socio-economic order needs them to be, when you can persuade them to be this for themselves while imagining it to be their free choice? Making good choices becomes an act of self-definition, but also a kind of self-censoring.

Free choice is implausible when offered without freedom from other constraints. Free choice is a burden in a neoliberal take-your-chances climate. And it is more apparent than real in the cloak of marketing opportunities that propose to us images of who we are and what we want.

## from polis to population

A NINETEENTH CENTURY innovation in the technology of surveillance was to place the guard tower at the center of the prison. In theory, now, the prisoners could be seen by the guards at any time. The design was used in many prisons throughout the British empire.

The notion of the "panopticon" is attributed to Jeremy Bentham, a founding father of liberalism. The innovation in the design went further than simplifying the work of the guards. It created a kind of self-policing. Fearing he was being watched, the prisoner censored his own actions, becoming his own jailer. This panopticon figures the way that, through the threat of surveillance, we are brought to conform.

The French historian Michel Foucault makes the panopticon into a motif of modern societies, in which whole populations police themselves according to norms they have internalized about what is appropriate behavior. This is how the public health discourse can become an instrument of population management to the end of social control rather than individual freedom. The surreptitious nudging of the public health campaign is not underwritten by the right of citizens to freely choose. Instead, it embodies a darker reality: the fading possibility of free choice in a world constructed by forces of persuasion.

Foucault elaborated the view that the growth of the modern governmentality produces subjects who fit their circumstances rather than individuals who create them. The public health discourse is just one of these actions on the populace working with the stealth of the iron hand in velvet glove. Foucault saw that the management of populations came down to aspects of our bodily comportment. He saw the fitness to work and the docility to accept our part in the social compact, however uneven, owed as much to whether we are adequately fed and housed, and whether our frailty in childhood and old age are accommodated, as it does to our rights and freedoms as liberal individuals.

Political philosophy was for the elite; it was "biopower" that drove the pistons of the social machine. Foucault deduced this not from how Everyman thought about himself and his situation, but from the way society dealt with his exceptions—the madman, the sexual deviant and the criminal. We can add to this list of social exceptions his wife and her child.

The "population" is not a creature of political philosophy but that of the social sciences—it marks the evolution from republic to society. In *The Human Condition*, Hannah Arendt describes this as the swallowing of the political realm by the social, and she makes a surprising critique of this development.

She observes in ancient Greece or Rome that the polis was the public realm, a place of characteristically human action to be contrasted with the private realm which was the place where the human as animal was cared for and bodily need ministered to. The unit of the private was the household, populated by women, children, slaves, and livestock—none of which had the status of citizen, but who were instead the (male) citizen's responsibility and his secluded fiefdom, aloof from political affairs.

But in the modern era, the "social" takes over the public realm and those functions that were previously distinguished from it in the private, according to Arendt. Feminism of the 1970s called out "the personal as political," drawing attention to the injustice harbored in the private sphere which had denied political action to all but the highest-born women. And yet, the becoming social of the political and its concomitant collapsing of public and private spheres is not, by Arendt's critique, the liberation that feminism sought. In fact, while injustice to women and many others has come to light in this evolution of the social sphere, its growing precedence has been rather to curtail that sphere of action for everyone.

Foucault's book *The Order of Things* is a diagnosis of the rise of the thinking of the social as a science, in which knowledge masters the subject (including the human subject) in a manner that parallels the capturing by technology of the human "standing reserve." *The Order of Things* was originally published in French as *Les Mots et les Choses*—words and things. The French title captures how the naming, labeling, and classifying of things make them "what they are," while the English title foregrounds knowledge as a *force majeure*.

Take, as an example of the making of one thing into another, the evolution of "the domestic" into "domestic violence"—and from there into "family violence." This is not trivial. Assault has always been a crime, but previously "the domestic" was a category of assault that police left well alone. A man was apparently entitled, by some strange feudal lien, to beat his wife and children in the privacy of their own home.

But at a certain point in the expanding jurisdiction of human rights, this behavior came to be regarded as anathema to the well-ordered state: "domestic violence" came out of the home and into the public discourse of health and welfare. The probable causes of this relate to all those changes that aim at normalizing the presence of men and women in the public sphere—including the emphasis on the category of "discrimination."

Why are women now being inducted into overt citizenship in this way? These messages take place parallel with the outlawing of race hate speech and homophobic violence. It is not, perhaps, the primary intent of the system to make life more pleasant for minorities. But it clearly obstructs productivity if certain categories of labor are excluded from contributing to the common wealth purely because of social norms that no longer are economically adaptive. The system needs everyone to work, just as it needs everyone to consume; capitalism is "gender-blind" and indifferent to race.

In the case of domestic violence, in particular, it becomes a matter of interest to the wider economic order if human capital is confined to the private serfdom of a particular man. The administration of the mandated change in these norms is given to public health and welfare bureaucracy to implement, through the legal mechanisms of definition and regulation. The renaming of the category from "domestic violence" to "family violence" extends the policy purview to the new generation.

The law is the classic form of power in writing. The text of the law has a special status, very often described as an Act. The direction of social policy might be charted in "law reform" that redefines aspects of unruly life under new orderings.

This bureaucracy can be contrasted with casuistry, which builds its knowledge from repeated experience of practice. In bureaucracy, the movement is in the other direction, from the principle to the particulars classified under it as actual events in time. The bureaucratic description of a future possibility is an act of the highest invention. This is why the production of "policy" is a struggle, to articulate unruly life as the operation in practice of an underlying principle.

Some things have become a great deal more complicated in the bureaucratic schematizing of unruly life: take the inflammatory area of "sexual harassment" recently re-ignited by the #metoo movement. The wolf-whistle previously appeared to some, in everyday casuistry, to be the expression of sexual approval of a woman in public. It now becomes "harassment" because it reduces the situation to one of sexual objectification. Sexual objectification is seen, according to principle, to conflict with the presence together of persons in the workplace with working roles and responsibilities.

It clearly is an intrusion into the routines of people working together to invoke this other ethos, of sexual predation. But some people (men, usually) find the new principle incomprehensible—it obstructs feelings that elsewhere they pursue unthinkingly in relating sexually to the world. Their feeling has suddenly become illegitimate, despite their experiencing it. This is not a defense of the man who thinks there's "no harm in admiring a pretty girl," nor of the many offenses of men who misuse the idea of sexism to assert "men's rights." It is to point to how the effort to cloak future undisclosed events in a prior reading of their meaning could struggle to succeed. It will, in certain ways, fail because "life" will exceed it.

But once the law underwrites this schematizing, the errant sexual action is called illegal, and people must learn to redefine their experience accordingly. The redefinition of experiences by the bureaucratic is a continuing invention. The growing edge of policy is into the various areas of experience that have previously been experienced under different possibilities, and given different names. In the case of the #metoo testimonies, the power of this social realm can be seen in an overwhelming amplification through social media. The potential of social media to exemplify the social realm, as Arendt conceives it, might give us pause. While sexual exploitation is an illegitimate use of influence, the trying of its crimes in the court of social media can be a rough sort of justice.

And then, in the bureaucratic ordering of everyday life some things have become a great deal simpler: today I can apply for a divorce online, ticking a few boxes, providing less information than when applying for a credit card and simply paying the all-important fee.

The *Family Law Act 1975* established the principle of no-fault divorce in Australian law. A similar measure is in place in other jurisdictions. This means that a court does not consider why the marriage has ended. The only grounds for divorce is that the marriage has broken down irretrievably. This is defined as there being "no reasonable likelihood" that the couple will reconcile and get back together. Couples must have been separated for at least twelve months and one day in order to satisfy the court that the marriage has broken down irretrievably.

No-fault divorce means there is no comeback from the other party except to plead an error of fact—for example, that there has been no separation. If one party says there is irretrievable breakdown, then hasn't there already been so? It's your word against mine.

The rising prevalence of divorce in modern societies charts a trajectory of the social realm through the private. The breaking of kinship in mid-generation was a social catastrophe in Europe in the late nineteenth century, and remains so today in traditional societies. But by the end of the twentieth century, it had become a credible life choice in the West.

This, and other more obviously technological means, have produced a revolution in categories that have previously governed the private sphere—in kinship, marriage, and reproduction.

## family values

THE SINGLE MOTHER is a figure of ambivalent political currency, of latent reproductive power.

The single mother is an exception that proves the rule. She is the technology of patriarchy seen from its other side. The single mother, conceiving or raising her children outside the structure that distributes social value across generations, was previously vilified or pitied because of it. She represented a variety of negatives; as the abandoned wife or jilted lover, she signified a man's truancy, the failure to do his duty. Or, as the sexual truant herself, she represented an unacceptable autonomy for women's desire.

As a mother she was historically problematic, because the maternal is dependent in patriarchal law, having no economic sphere of its own. The question was: Who will support her, and, as significantly, her child? She marked the failure of a technology of reproduction, the weak link in its chain of patriarchal relations that binds generations together, and families to other families, in a civil society.

Single mothers may carry a stigma they don't deserve. They are asked to cover over the collapse of the patriarchal arrangement, in a deeply sexist bargain that they have the worst of. They carry the failure of the sexual revolution to free women from reproductive burdens. Yet many single mothers, by definition, demonstrate a preference for the autonomy of wages, however low, or for living on the pension even where it brings hardship, over the numbness of a moribund marriage or the terror of an abusive one. Patriarchy doesn't work for everyone.

The sole parent pension might be seen as payment for the labor of reproducing the society—a minimal and pitiful payment, but a cash value nevertheless put on labor that, under patriarchy, was donated in return for favor and protection. The housewife might conventionally take care of the children, keep house and make food and clothing, taking care of "family life" 24/7. But still, when asked at a party "do you work?" she would have replied: "Oh no! I'm just a housewife."

The question of women's work has increasingly involved a "double-think" as well as the "double day." As an employee, her work is called labor and she is entitled to the same rights that give male workers living wages, negotiated conditions, and collective bargaining power or marketable skill value.

In contrast, as a mother and wife, her work is not only "never done," but inherently invisible. There is no basic wage, no forty-eight-hour week, overtime, penalty rates, paid holiday and sick leave, no separation entitlements, severance pay nor superannuation. Of course, there is alimony in the case of divorce, and the presumption she will inherit from her husband their joint property in the event of his death.

The double think—that productive work is labor, but reproductive work, including gestation labor, is not labor—is a consequence of the industrial-bourgeois revolutions. Marx may argue that "men made clothes for years, before any became a tailor." But in fact, it was a woman who made clothes for subsistence; the tailor was a man. Engels saw this very early, that the private sphere was run along different lines than the labor market, and he also saw that it operated to the economic disadvantage of women and children.

Yet there was a certain stability in the arrangement, while men were heads of households and were paid a "working man's wage"; that is, one that allowed for the cost of providing for dependents, too. Wage cases from early in the twentieth century show courts explicitly reasoning around these obligations in setting a living wage.

And the work of men in the newly industrialized world could be dirty, repetitive, monotonous, and dangerous. Labor is work per unit time, and selling one's labor is selling one's time. In Marx's eyes, it was a Faustian deal that took one's life under pretext of sustaining it. At least the worker's wife could still do her tasks in her own time and according to her own lights. And working for love must often have been more enriching than working for money.

The welfare state, as enacted for example in the UK act of 1945, marked an historical change in arrangements that, following reforms like the *Married Women's Property Act* and universal suffrage, indicates the emergence of modernity in the fortunes of the family. It took upon the government the paternal role; it substituted the state for the father in many matters, and in so doing, changed patriarchy.

It had never previously been possible for those of his subjects who were fathers to abdicate their paternal responsibilities to the Crown. But the welfare state allowed the burden of paternity to shift from individual men to the state itself, and in this reversal we might see foreshadowed the diminishing potency of the patriarchal. It initiated fears of the "nanny state," a population orphaned, and a cascading concern over the "feminizing" of power, including characterizing the ever-growing bureaucracy as a maternal stifling of the virile body politic. The making public of this private responsibility promoted the state over the family in some senses, and changed the technology of reproduction subtly but radically. We are still feeling the different currents of this change surging around us—we don't yet know what it will (re)produce.

As the private sphere was in effect "collectivized" under the aegis of the welfare state, it also became necessary to political economy that the private sphere consume. The private sphere became not just the place of reproduction, set off from the public sphere of production; it became the site of consumption. And this consumer society emerging with the welfare state post-war was driven by a voracious economic order that demanded greater and greater consumption—exponential growth, not a mere sustainable stasis. The trajectory of late-stage capitalism, wherever it may lead, is an accelerating one. That speed now keeps both sexes working in the labor force to sustain family life. Yet the statistics show that, despite more than fifty years of the consumer economy and of the sexual revolution, the bulk of housework and childcare still falls to women.

Since the 1970s, feminists were diagnosing a structural problem for women's rights, disguised as they were in the half-light of the private sphere. While consumption has been brought into the public glare, acknowledged along with production as a critical element in the political economy of the nation, reproduction remains obscured, largely unfunded and still donated by women to the polity out of her leisure and personal well-being. It's striking how little this injustice has been redressed, despite the talk-show phenomena of labor-saving devices and stay-at-home dads.

Indeed, while consumer technology undoubtedly has speeded up the time taken to perform some household tasks, no-fault divorce has created an explosion of one-parent households, very largely single mothers and their children, living at risk of poverty and with the stress of emotional and financial hardship. It has also produced the phenomenon of second and even third families drawing on the male's earning power.

## reproducing the family

WILL THE FAMILY survive the twenty-first century? There are conflicting signs. Conflicting because, in some ways, "family values" are more potent than ever, at least for raising political capital. The swing to more social conservatism has characterized the past decades; it is more politically correct now than it ever was to refer to the fundamental social value that the family gives to modern life; the importance of supporting it ideologically and financially.

And fifty years after the sexual revolution, it is still the case that the family remains the unit of measurement in the social imaginary. At the same time, demographics show us that this is an ideal honored as much in the breach. One-person households, de facto, divorced and single parents with children, retired people, blended families, gay couples, and DINKS (double income no kids)—these are all recognizable forms of a household if they are still not presented as the norm. No doubt they already outnumber the norm.

These alternatives to the ideal operate as cartographic insets (the image is Moira Gatens') in a basic plan of the social world in which family means nuclear family, of husband and wife and pigeon pair. Why is this formation still so significant in our imaginations, when the lived experience of the majority of us differs from it? Does our commitment to it show that we are nostalgic for a treasured relic that is decomposing? Or will it prove to be a sentiment that lags behind, but supports, a mutating of the family toward something else as yet unimagined?

"I'd rather have a beer than win Father of the year," sings Homer Simpson, the suburban Everyman, revealing as usual a truth of our times; that masculinity and fatherhood are often seen as competing values. Being with the guys, "among men," is different from being a good father, and indeed, to be a good father may even show you to be unmanly, as Ned Flanders bears out. We could go so far as to say that conformity to patriarchal obligation is not a marker of masculinity. In fact, it is sometimes the rule-breaker, the larrikin, the loner or the maverick that signifies the masculine in defiance of the father figure. So, masculinity is not the same thing as patriarchy.

The battle of the sexes is not the point then, for the future of the family. Equality for women hasn't been achieved merely by making them the peers of their brothers and cousins, the men of their generation. Sexual politics is more intricate than this, since, although the nuclear family looks like it is about husbands and wives, it is in effect a triangulated structure in which the leading term is "father." The figure of the father represents the family in many senses of this word. Traditionally the head of the household, it was the father who owned the property, exercised the vote, and so on. The father represented the family in the sense of symbolizing, but also by acting in its name. The role of father, which necessarily implies a man having progeny, marks the key relation of the family as a cross-generational entity.

In a strange, complicated, and conflicted way, fatherhood is optional where motherhood is not. Men are praised for aspiring to the status, while women are assumed to be unlikely to escape it. As the saying goes: it's a wise child that knows its father. The child's mother is necessarily present at the birth, but witnessing paternity involves more: the infant's hereditary characteristics were observed for millennia before scientists tested for DNA. But still the causal chain is less immediately felt than the visceral connection holding together a woman and her infant.

As anthropologists have analyzed, marriage brings together and makes kin of people who were not born of the same mothers or fathers. Most marriage rules function to provoke families to intermarry, by preserving their property and cultural capital in the process, if not increasing it. So, for example, in Australian Aboriginal society, my relation to my mother's skin group would confer membership of one kind of cultural law, and of my father's skin group another. I am enriched by this "exogamy," as the anthropologists call it, rather than dispossessed by it, in the coming together of different family lines in me. In contemporary Western culture, marrying you gives me some sort of claim on your property, and certainly, conveys a strong claim over it to our children. Inheritance preserves social standing and cultural membership across generations.

We look on being related as just the same thing as having a "biological tie." But marriage is the large exception in present first-world arrangements. While paternal lineage preserves biological kin between the generations, the avoidance of incest dictates a non-biological tie in the present one. The family in the contemporary world is still organized according to a patriarchal principle in which blood relation to the father governs kinship from one generation to the next, while "all-but" blood relations can become kin in the same generation by marriage. It is through the father's bloodline, and not the mother's, that I am identified by name, and it is through avoiding a certain proximity as incestuous (by not marrying blood relations) that who I can marry is determined. Although marked by biology, this kinship is not biological; it is conventional.

Our form of the family seems so natural that it can be hard to imagine things otherwise. Having a mother and father who were themselves in the prescribed relationship of marriage is seen as a baseline. But actually, this arrangement is already a kind of kinship that is highly specialized to the task of reproducing late industrial society, and involves several intricacies and reversals on other arrangements. In other societies and within subgroups different possibilities emerge—from harems to matrilineal clans.

For example, we may no longer need monogamy. The structure had meaning before contraception, when the family was the premier reproductive technology. It protected the stakeholders in the family before women could work meaningfully outside the home. When the male breadwinner was supporting a household of dependents, the family couldn't permit rivals for his resources, unless he was wealthy—and even then, there was the succession to be protected. He needed to be sure he was paying to support his own children and not someone else's.

Monogamy has its roots in the species-need to bear and raise young who take many years of care to bring to maturity. This species-need has not gone away—arguably children need a longer period of care and learning than ever to cope with the demands of a complicated technological society. But there are other ways to bring up children than inside monogamous marriage, as many couples find out post-divorce.

Care for the children of a marriage is still a somewhat asymmetrical burden, often falling harder on mothers than fathers. But marriage is no longer the monolithic structure outside of which childrearing cannot be imagined. Women's rights, their increased economic independence, and a rise in the acceptance of childcare outside the home has changed all this.

While the social need for monogamy is changing, perhaps, the psychological need for sexual fidelity from a partner may seem more enduring. And maybe this isn't surprising since a large part of our emotional makeup might not be instrumental at all. Self-interest and species-interest conflict, and especially around the conditions of care provided to other generations. The finely calibrated social arrangements given to the care of both the young and the old are not simply instrumental despite being driven by function. They call on feelings of compassion for others, altruism and the need to care as crucial survival values.

## reproducing technology

THEY ARE CALLED the ARTs—assisted reproductive technologies. Or maybe, artificial reproductive technologies. This is in contrast to natural reproductive technologies, presumably, which means sex.

Many jurisdictions have now set up a voluntary register for the recording of the identity of sperm donors and children born of donors. The social changes that have led to such a roll call are remarkable, and they seem to represent the most artificial of the ARTs; the uniting of egg and sperm in people who have never met.

Donor insemination has found a market because of a most natural desire, that of a couple to have a child of the union. And the roll call has become necessary because the sperm donor was originally anonymous. The identity of the biological father has until recently been suppressed in the service of the heterosexual marital bond and its reproduction. The rights of paternity to these offspring have been given to the husband, although he is more technically in the place of a stepfather.

Yet who really is the father in this circumstance? This modern man has initiated the pregnancy with his partner, has seen it through birth and infancy, raised the child from the first nappy changed through to the first driving lesson. How much more can one ask of a father? How much more authentically can someone be related to someone else than through this everyday—sometimes repetitive, sometimes inspiring—practice of love? It's hard to see how the addition of one half of the genes is more than a recondite curiosity in comparison.

The possibility of donor insemination—not a complicated procedure technologically—is one of a group of ART interventions that can allow same-sex couples, infertile women, and those with age or other medical complications to have their own children.

For traditionalists, the idea of reproductive technology may feel uncomfortable—and in questions of the family, feelings are critical. They are relied on to keep the social structure in place. Shame may be felt where family members couple "inappropriately," that is, against the norms whatever those may be. From social snobbery to honor killing, the potency of the social reproductive system to sustain its laws works through schooling our emotions.

Affects are a primary and archaic source of judgment and action. We learned them "at our mother's knee." Feelings of pride and shame are harnessed to ideas of what is natural and unnatural by the time we go to school. They intensify throughout adolescence, and by the time we are adult, may be so fixed as to constitute a knockdown argument for us on family matters. The sentiment, "it doesn't feel right," "it's just not natural," becomes uncritically respected as a ground for judgment and action on social arrangements, and even as a defense to violence.

Maybe for centuries there was no need to question, merely to follow, these intuitions that allowed each to find their place in the patriarchy. Maybe we wouldn't question it today, except that certain things that seemed "unnatural" or irregular regularly keep happening, and other things that seemed "natural" are falling away.

The current growing edge of the ARTs extends to the more ethically charged question of surrogacy, the agreement of a woman to carry someone else's genetic child to term for money. In most jurisdictions, including in some developing nations, this is presently not lawful and held to be against public policy.

Thailand, for example, moved against the practice after the case of "Baby Gammy," one of twins born to a surrogate from Australian parents. Baby Gammy was born with Downs syndrome. The couple took delivery of his sister, who was a healthy baby, and returned to Australia, but they declined to adopt Baby Gammy who was left with the surrogate. A more naked example of the dangers of commodifying the field is hard to find. It was made more disturbing by the historical convictions against the father for child sexual abuse; news reports had it that he was having the children merely for sexual access. This gained attention for a moral panic around unscrupulous pedophilia rings, and the possibility of their access to ARTs.

But perhaps the commodifying of offspring is a more general scandal. Perhaps the introduction of the instrumental in the field throws into relief our commonplace urges in respect of the right way to have children.

The great challenge to the family is technology. This proposition may not startle; it might even seem at first glance to be banal. Of course technology is a challenge given the disruptive potential of IVF, stem cell research, and cloning. From another perspective, it will be dismissed as familiar doom-saying—the family, it might be said, is essential to our human nature, and technology will never defeat it because humans will always need the family.

Natural and essential? Or archaic and threatened? The challenge for thinking about it will be to envisage what of that traditional order will mutate, what will sustain itself, and what will decompose.

As I have argued elsewhere—in *Copula*: *Sexual Technologies Reproductive Powers*—it is through technology, in the variety of its means and ends, that we are instructed in desires that are not natural or not found in nature. Technology as a new kind of order challenges the natural order that the family made of things previously. And technology as expressive of an instrumental order challenges an older kind of family bond and the relation of care embodied in it. The context in which this strangeness arises weighs on convictions about human life and love, convictions governed by the paradox of relations between ourselves and others.

## mother love

A TAX ACCOUNTANT would tell you that childcare may not be tax-deductible because it is a private expense, like clothing, transport to and from work and housing. Ironically, because everyone is deemed to incur these expenses, then in some jurisdictions it is not regarded as an expense occurred specifically to gain income.

The Tax Commissioner may concede that the taxation system is one arm of social policy, and that the decision not to permit deductions for some private expenses arises from the prohibitive cost it would put on the economy. And anyway, to do so would be a kind of double counting, because the rate of wages is structured around the cost of living that all workers face. Despite buying time as labor, the cost of the future is not borne by enterprise in general. The cost of reproduction continues to pose as a personal and not as an economic one.

Childcare has a long history, from Plato's nurseries as proposed in the *Republic*, to the contemporary childcare center. The variety of arrangements adopted include the wet nurse, live-in nanny, boarding school, the orphanage, the extended family, and abbreviating childhood through child labor. But the greater dimension that the child's own family is thought to bring to their care has always been valued, since love is the surest way of binding and belonging. The infant and the young child, in their trustingness and need, put very clearly before the eyes of a loving parent the bare needs of childrearing that can be so conveniently veiled in social work and policy. Children seek love to inspire their efforts to grow.

And not just a bland bureaucratic love, extended to all as a matter of policy, but the genuine bond incited by this child in their singularity, and by the stake that the carer has in its flourishing. Love like this is not mass-produced. It is a cottage industry, modeled on the physical proximity of the mother's body from before birth when the child is enveloped in it.

This relation is so crucial to human development that many psychologists have regarded it as definitive of our species. Born helpless and suckled by its mother, the human child is in need of protection for many years. It is nominally twelve years before he takes up the dignity of initiation in many societies. Eighteen years in technological society before she is customarily regarded as able to enter into the rights, freedoms and obligations of being a citizen. Each of these eighteen years relies on loving relations with others to meet the physical, emotional, and intellectual needs of growth. Expensive. And maybe you can't buy it, the love of someone for whom your well-being is an intimate part of their own.

This affective aspect of the family, this love for kin, helps to explain why technological society struggles with the question of dependence. It explains why, despite the welfare state, the consumer mentality, and the national economy, the public and the social spheres have not completely been able to digest the private. There is a deep contradiction between the figure of the technologized modern citizen-consumer, and the facts of life demonstrated in the effort of reproducing this figure. A free agent, responsible only for himself, he disavows the agency of the others who raised him through the years he could not be such. The adult citizen owes a debt, but one that this politics pretends is a donation. Just as the free men of democratic Athens were supported by a behind-the-scenes cast of women and slaves, so the democrat of today can still not make good on the promise of universal autonomy.

Our species life is not yet like that. Could it ever be? Would the love of a mother as simulated by a virtual reality program nevertheless produce authentic emotional growth in a child? Would a society that was trained to provide for its own interests and desires exclusively, only doing for others transactionally that which coincided with those interests and desires, hang together as a society? Or would it tear itself apart?

## natality

THE WORLD'S POPULATION is greater than at any other time in species history. But this crisis remains largely in the realm of social medicine and out of the purview of political philosophy while it is thought as the idea of "populations." To meet the world of mass population with an alternative to the bureaucracy of health economists, who make policy on birth control within the passive context of the administration of public health and medical care, requires finding a political articulation of that world. And it needs to find it in the face of a contrary motion toward the digital abstraction of the populace in social media and artificial intelligence.

Feminist philosophers are now re-reading Hannah Arendt, and taking up her concept of "natality" as a way of addressing this. Hannah Arendt's thinking on natality is framed within her work in a sustained meditation on how totalitarian politics came to be. She regarded the totalitarian governments of National Socialism and Stalinist communism to be a new form of government that could only come to pass in a world of mass populations—in the twentieth century, in the wake of industrial-technological revolution.

The idea of "natality" as outlined by Arendt in *The Human Condition* lies uniquely on the border between social, public and private, and occurs not as a biological but as a political event.

> Labor and work, as well as action, are . . . rooted in natality in so far as they have the task to provide and preserve the world for, to foresee and reckon with, the constant influx of newcomers who are born into the world as strangers. However of the three, action has the closest connection with the human condition of natality; the new beginning inherent in birth can make itself felt in the world only because the newcomer possesses the capacity of beginning something anew, that is, of acting. (1958, 9)

In their recent analysis, *Arendt, Natality and Biopolitics*, Rosalyn Diprose and Ewa Ziarek write: "it is not simply that 'natality' is the result of an individual aptitude or specific human faculty (for example, of mind). A human being is a new beginning by virtue of their 'appearance' in the sociohistorical world and, whatever the person is doing, their actions begin something new in the sense that they have a unique and unpredictable effect on others and on the course of events" (2019, 5).

This is important to take up, especially in the "mass" era when each of us can now be thought as "only one of seven billion." The digital over-emphasizes the faculty of mind and abstracts human being, which despite this, is immersed in its material necessity and its physical frailty, dwelling in the life span between a birth and a death.

"Arendt suggests that the 'capacity of beginning something new' through action and speech is inseparable from the condition of community (the 'presence of other human beings') and human plurality," they argue.

Being born into a world with others becomes seen as the ground of individual being, and gives conceptual strength to the idea of "natality." It prevents from the outset the conceiving of human life as either simply biological or simply as a metaphysics of the individual. Sociality is primary. We can see the pertinence of this conception now, in an era of false individualism that sees its expression only in terms of the consumer's free choice; and at the same time, of strident identity politics crying out for distinctions without real differences—in which plurality is reduced merely to so many brands.

This conception of natality also matters, this being in company with others, when we regard its shadow, the isolation invoked in the breakdown of community. The transition to the urban has disrupted customary identities, and thrust new generations onto a path of globalized futures. But these vistas aren't always realistic, while the lived reality of the rupture can leave people with atomized lives that are lived primarily alone. The global village as an ideal is far from the high-rise dormitories and urban environments of many modern cities. It is interesting to take up Arendt's remarks on loneliness, in part three of *Origins of Totalitarianism*, as a political effect of totalitarian rule in this context.

"[T]he event of 'natality' can be understood as the unique philosophical concept that Arendt adds to political theory to explain the play of the conditioned and unconditioned that underlies human existence and hence to explain the 'principle' underlying democracy," write Diprose and Ziarek.

This articulation of democracy seems more than ever germaine, in a context dominated by, on the one hand, impotent partisan political parties and on the other, rising populist groups. Neither of these candidates for power are representative of the plurality Arendt enunciates in this ethic of the natal.

Through "natality," Arendt is interpreted as delivering concepts of power, freedom, and alliance that overcome two stumbling blocks in alternative modern political theories: on the one hand, the view of power that rules out change by political agency, often attributed to Foucault. On the other, the negative freedom of social contract theorists that leaves only individual rights under the protection of governance.

In engaging the power to "make live and let die" with the question of the political actor, Diprose and Ziarek open up some urgent questions; the rise of right-wing nationalist politics, the intensifying of alienation in contemporary urban life, and the reverses suffered by women in relation to their reproductive rights despite being citizens of apparently liberal democratic states.

It's as well to remember Arendt formulates her philosophy from her experience as a Jewish refugee with firsthand knowledge of Nazism. Her anxiety about the bureaucratic caused her to describe it as a regressive agent that made the political sphere into the private/social through the administration of populations. This locates the unique positioning of "natality" on the border between public and private, and not as a biological but as a political event.

Because a new beginning by definition has an unpredictable impact on the world, governments are inclined to control human birth as part of wider regulation of so-called "biological life." Of particular concern to contemporary gender politics is the argument that the social process of normalization is on a conceptual continuum with the lethal governance of totalitarian forms. The insight presses on the very real dismay we might feel at the way in which political collective action of the mid- to late- twentieth century has dissipated into "distinctions without difference" that drive social identities across the political spectrum. It sketches why the granting of political recognition is not enough to protect specific groups from discrimination. In *Origins of Totalitarianism*, Arendt analyses, in an intricate mapping, the precursors to totalitarian government in the imperialism of the nineteenth century and the rise of the social sphere of "making live and letting die."

The perspective in which we imagine reproduction as a philosophical event is strikingly novel. It is perhaps a view that can only come to light in the creation of a different kind of philosopher—one with a proximity to the bodily realm of sexuality and gender, and to giving birth and child-rearing. This space has previously been conceived of as not philosophical, as not a place for the deliberation of public affairs. And yet, by stealth, the space is colonized as biopower if not given voice as political speech.

It seems clear that this "world of strangers," who will have been our descendants and for whom we will be ancestors, deserve better than this. It follows from these ardent reflections on Arendt's view of the human condition that democracy needs to be "re-conceived."

THE VALUE OF CHOICE, in neoliberal hands, becomes a feint of self-assertion in a world governed increasingly by population control and mass consumerism.

Foucault is an insistent observer of the engineering of the populace including into units of subjective experience. The larger-than-life figure of the panopticon still remains one of the best for understanding it. The organizing of unruly life under the auspices of health, welfare and family law graphically illustrate a system that compels individual choice to affirm an overwhelming matrix of determining practices.

But the life of the family is many-faceted, and the role of choice in it becomes constrained not only by objective structures but also by the feelings which provide its subjective reinforcement. Reproduction is at once the most public and the most private good.

It is Arendt who observes a totalitarian edge to bureaucratic power, and brings this into focus for us in the realm of the social. Through Arendt's category of "natality," a new biopolitics can be seen to critique the collapse of the public and private spheres into the social.

*[seven]*

# *[free love]*

ON A PARIS bridge, a tradition of lovers' locks has sprung up. Each couple places a padlock through the grating and closes it, abandoning the key to the Seine. The locks commemorate the loving bond and a romantic pledge. The holding of oneself to a bond with someone else, committing oneself "come what may" to the captivity of the lock without the key, enacts the padlock as a symbol of binding for better or worse. Who knows how many locks are later on removed when, in our contemporary fickle world, the bond is dissolved?

Our desires are fodder for the culture industry; pushed into the shape of something that can be addressed as consumable—from the soap opera to the cosmetics counter—and sold back to us. The narratives into which we channel desire are governed by social determinations about permissible bondings and illicit couplings. Our judgments on ourselves are governed, at least in part, by how we're valued by others "in the market."

And desire is now morphing under the pressures of the technological and the digital, to remake online our most personal adventures in intimacy, and to make them mean something. What are the consequences of commodifying the need for sexual and other companionship? Is sex a commodity, and romance something you find off-market? Or can you find love on the internet, on internet dating sites, and through virtual sex?

From dating agencies and social media to internet porn, the connection between self and other is presented as increasingly transactional. Instrumentalism is a large part of how people are taught to think about love. It might be thought that love and internet commerce ought to be opposed; that love being a unique and irrational epiphany is at the other end of a spectrum of commodified interchangeable products.

But actually as it turns out love is the ideal commodity, perfect for the internet, perfect for the age. This is not because you can buy love, but because the commodity is already a species of love. Love is a reification of an object, the value-adding of a projection.

The commodity is the ultimate love relation, the perfect projection of value in solid form. Specifically, love is the psychological operation of binding something outside myself to myself by means of its image. There is a parallel action seen in the commodity, which defines things according to their images, parcelling them up as potential means of satisfaction.

The paradox is that "free love" is an oxymoron—there is nothing free about love because however temporary, transactional, or exploitative, love is by definition a tie. Love that was not so would not satisfy, since even before love, which is a demand addressed to the world, desire is itself a question put to "the other." At the same time, love is a unique relation, one that distills the object-relations that give us our psychical place in things.

## Ashley Madison

NEW ROLES OFFERED in the virtuality of the internet illustrate the place of desire in its transmission. The idea of free love with no strings attached—the gratification of desire in the present which has no future consequences—is a strong fantasy in an instrumental age.

It may be a naïve expression of instrumental thinking faced with our emotional needs and desires. It doesn't work completely. But in many ways people can get partial satisfaction from fantasy. The idea of love as a commodity, and of sexual desire and desire for companionship as things that can be bought online, is embodied in the internet dating site.

"Life is short. Have an affair." The slogan for the Ashley Madison website only means something in the light of marriage which, as in institution, generally implies sexual fidelity. The advice to have an affair may be ethically dubious, an adjuration to "cheat."

The affair of Ashley Madison is instructive; the internet dating site proposed transgressing the traditional love/care relation in the instrumental type to "have a bit on the side," and to have it virtually, promising to be a diversion from that reality as a simpler mode of relating to love-objects.

For some, having an affair is a way to survive the claustrophobia of monogamy. It's the exception designed to prove the rule—when it's over, he goes back to his wife. But having affairs is a high-risk game, because infidelity that comes to light in a monogamous relationship tends to provoke a crisis in it. The chaste partner is often irretrievably wounded and feels the whole basis of the partnership is undermined. And the end of the affair can presage the end of the marriage for the unfaithful partner too, who may not be able to go back to an exclusivity that is no longer satisfying. (Laura Kipnis offers a compelling account of this in *Against Love*: *A Polemic.*)

Ashley Madison made themselves famous for a breach of internet security that brought down this fantasy for many thousands of consumers. In an extortion attempt that saw the site hacked in 2015, thousands of anonymous clients were threatened with exposure. It was okay while these links remained virtual. It was really not okay when they were forced into the light of day; where husbands and wives discovered they were not alone together in their coupledom, but instead had a third party involved on the internet.

The fantasy was revealed as wishful thinking, once the website was hacked and the virtual guarantee was lost. This was the extreme malfunction of a situation that is common: the virtual as a parallel reality, one that our psychology does not distinguish from the real thing. The romance takes place as a kind of dissociation that distorts our relations of love and care.

In the case of the parent company, Toronto-based Avid Life Media, Ashley Madison's business model was based on this unrealistic desire for a virtual swinging community, and was doubly cynical since the promise of sex and suggestive come-ons was more often generated by algorithms that could "part lustful men from hundreds of dollars within minutes of logging on" as Claire Brownell reported in the *Financial Post* of September 11, 2015:

> One of the former customer service representatives estimated that just under one-third of the calls that came in were from female members. But because the ratio was far from even, the company looked for ways to keep men messaging and chatting, and spending.

A lawsuit from several thousand claimants following the breach was settled out of court for $11.2 million. Staff at the business, who were bound by a nondisclosure agreement that extended well after their employment ended, nevertheless spoke to the reporter about the harrowing calls received from irate wives and devastated children declaring: "You've ruined our family, I hope you're happy, my mommy's crying, it's all your fault."

Clients of Ashley Madison were manipulated in an excruciating reversal of the instrumental relationship they themselves had sought. The instrumentalism was reversed in an ironic twist that saw male clients taken advantage of by the company itself. Claire Brownell reports that many thousands of the female profiles on the site showed signs of being unattached to real women, while leaked internal documents from the company appear to suggest that computer algorithms were used to generate some of the flirtatious responses to eager men. This was widely known among Ashley Madison staff. It was even alleged that profile photos were taken from the free-licensing area of the photo-hosting service Flickr or from deactivated accounts.

Multiple former employees alleged that, while the company had initially employed live "chat hostesses" to engage the men, in time they replaced the live workers with computerized bots. As the *Financial Post* editorialized: "That would mean that Ashley Madison's bots could effectively pass the famous 'Turing test' for artificial intelligence—where a human could not detect even after a few questions that he was talking to a machine and not another person."

In the "Turing test" for artificial intelligence a version of a parlor game called the "Imitation Game" is imagined. A person and a machine, hidden behind a door and unobservable to the player, provide answers to questions that are intended to persuade the player that they are a human respondent. Turing's point was that should a machine deceive the player into thinking it was human, then "intelligence" was shown to be not just a human capacity.

It may not be incidental that Turing's original parlor game was one in which the players hiding behind the door were each trying to deceive the others as to whether they were a man or a woman. Even at the outset, it seems, the search for artificial intelligence was mixed up with sex.

## artificial intimacy

"CYBORG BRIDES" ran the headline.

"Sex robot creator Sergi Santos says people will marry his creations within the next 20 years—and claims he's worked out how to have a BABY with one"—British tabloid *The Sun* carried this classic media "beat-up" that played on the scandal of instrumental sex, at the same time as plumbing the depths of social mythology about marital sex, in October 2017.

Sergi Santos and his partner Maritsa Kissamitaki market their "advanced" sex dolls for £2,000–£5,000 each from their location in Catalonia, Spain. The robots are an output of an artificial intelligence project that is hyped as bringing potentially huge profits from a forecast of the changes technology might make to intimate relations. "The Spanish scientist believes that it's only a matter of time before human and robot marriage is commonplace."

But first, to make the marketing palateable, the couple appear regularly in the press peddling several messages about the product masquerading as science fantasy: that the AI doll can be a believable substitute for a sexual partner; that the relationship had with the doll can be felt as attachment (she "enjoys" sex, we are told) and; that despite this, the real world spouse need not feel threatened because their marital relationship after all is "built on mutual trust and respect."

Santos is quoted as claiming the dolls allow him to satisfy his sex drive without going outside the marriage, at the same time as he speculates on a future in which the AI doll could become a surrogate spouse and even produce a robotic child substitute. Meanwhile, Kissamitaki ponders the amusing technical challenges of creating a male version of the doll. Were she to use it, her husband declares, it would make him "jealous."

In an extended report on Barcroft TV, the "problem" that the AI sex robot is designed to solve is couched in terms of providing sexual satisfaction for couples who might otherwise divorce. This social mission (which the pair claim might also "help the lonely and the socially awkward") is no doubt intended to retro-fit the salacious headlines with the reassuring normalcy of heterosexual marital desires. In short, the sex robot, like porn and other stimulants, is a way of enhancing the experience of masturbation.

*The Sun* also reports on the UK's first sex doll "brothel" opened in London in 2018 (The Dolly Parlour, £50 for half an hour) and the Chinese prototype being developed that will also turn on the dishwasher and laugh at its owner's jokes. It is not yet a runaway market—RealDoll.com (which has populated the brothel) claims to sell only about 400 dolls a year.

The futuristic fantasy gives way to an old-fashioned reality—"sexologists warn we run the risk of becoming addicted to artificial intelligence lovemaking," opines *The Sun's* psychological expert. "Sex addiction is a way to anaesthetize hard to bear feeling states" such as shame, boredom, and depression, and "sex with a robot is just a fake imitation," says the expert. "And it can lead to psychopathic disorders and isolation. Sex with robots won't bring into a person's life the emotion effect that gives us true communion."

Beneath this flummery, which no doubt even its intended audience interpret as something of a gag, lies the disturbing threat the robot and artificial intelligence pose to human being. Love is the limit case, because there is no aspect of object-relations as volatile and at the same time as likely to drive actions (such as taking out the credit card). Perhaps the AI sex doll is merely in the same category as dating sites like Ashley Madison, as a dodgy ruse to part the desirous from their money. And yet, the question the doll puts to the instrumental is a serious one. She asks: What of your desire for love is natural and part of being human, and what is artificial and capable of being gratified by simulacra?

In another documentary on sex dolls, "The Sex Robots Are Coming," an elderly male client is seen wheeling his life-sized doll—the simulacrum of a teenage blonde—in a stroller around the neighborhood, and dressing her, brushing her hair and performing other grooming tasks. His aging wife sits on the lounge with the doll, but it isn't clear how she understands her own role in this. The portrait is one of uncompromising despair.

What is happening to subjectivity trained in this feigned experience, both of sexual release but also of social fraud? It's hard to avoid the suspicion that punters are being asked to suspend disbelief in order to salve the malaise of failing heterosexual marriage and the loneliness of contemporary urban life.

## the imitation game

THE SEARCH FOR pleasure on the internet can easily reveal its underside, the search for relief from emotional pain.

While looking for love drives some to online dating sites, loneliness and alienation drive others to seek help in therapy. Web programs have grown up recently around the treatment of psychological conditions like depression. Yet the therapeutic relation may be even more difficult to commodify or take online than the sexual relation without seeming false.

Meanwhile, the labor of treating affective conditions, a burden that traditionally may have fallen to a parish priest or similar spiritual figure, is becoming expensive. The years of training of psychologists in a "talking cure" make the hourly rate prohibitive when billed *en masse* to the public health system.

Enter "Moodzone," a webpage on the NHS site that advocates the use of "self-help therapies." These are, it explains "psychological therapies that you can do in your own time to help with problems like stress, anxiety and depression. . . . They can be a useful way to try out a therapy like cognitive behavioral therapy (CBT) to see if it's for you."

The site adds that these therapies can also be convenient if "you're short of time, you have family or work commitments, you can't get out easily, you want a therapy that's completely anonymous," and so on.

Online treatments for depression like Moodzone raise the question of whether there is something manipulative in being drawn to confide online to a program that is simulating empathy and understanding. We might ask whether empathic responses are just a series of signs strung together like any other text, or whether there is something above and beyond the form of words being given and received in "real human interaction," and specifically in psychotherapy.

Behavioral psychology describes its subjects on the model of a kind of "bot"; it imagines human beings as a string of code that results in apparent action. The opposition at stake is that between authentic and inauthentic, and whether the Turing Test reduces the whole population of "other minds" to a believable simulation. The reason cognitive behavior therapy suits the Turing test is that it comes from the same model of other minds; that is, the idea that the other is a black box opaque to me and known only from its observable gestures. This is a profoundly instrumental model.

Any chatterbot can satisfy the test—the question this raises is where does it leave the human interlocutor? Whether he or she is being deceived about the responses being human, or the simulation is known to be supplied in lieu of human interaction, can a person really be said to be receiving the "same" gratification as from ordinary conversation? Or is this resistance nostalgia for an "anthropomorphic fallacy?"

If it makes no difference whether the confidante is really listening or is just a simulation of listening, then perhaps it would be possible that the need for care and empathy could be met online by a bot. This would have consequences for the urge for love and romance, and for sexual adventure too.

But this seems intuitively implausible. People report feeling deceived, when on dating websites correspondents are persuaded to pay over their savings to a phantom lover who turns out to be a Nigerian syndicate, or when in chatrooms they find that kids are being groomed for sexual abuse by pedophiles posing as peers. In some circumstances, offering to meet emotional need by simulation is more than artificial—it is deceptive (and criminal).

Or is the artificiality of the simulation more like masturbation or prostitution, which are venerable compensatory practices? Is the distinction between the real and the virtual illogical since once the exchange gets going it takes shape as a sign system like any other, where you read the social cues? Specifically in the case of sex, does a bodily presence to each other exceed its instrumental incidence as a set of signs?

In *Alone Together*, Sherry Turkle takes issue with an over-optimistic argument proffered by David Levy in his book *Love and Sex with Robots*. In response to Levy's argument there is "one simple criterion for judging the worth of robots in even the most intimate domains. Does being with a robot make you feel better?" She writes of being troubled at the thought of people "seeking intimacy with a machine that has no feelings, can have no feelings, and is really just a clever collection of 'as if' performances, behaving as if it cared, as if it understood us."

As a trained psychoanalyst, Turkle prizes authenticity which she describes as following from "the ability to put oneself in the place of another, to relate to the other because of a shared store of human experiences: we are born, have families, and know loss and the reality of death. A robot, however sophisticated, is patently out of this loop."

Turkle is surely right that the utilitarian principle of Levy's formulation misses the point of intimacy. But judging authenticity by shared content might also miss a richer engagement that intimacy implies. Beyond content, there is a synchrony in intimacy that arises from co-location, a transferential pleasure in being together by whatever means this takes place.

"Sociable robots serve as both symptom and dream: as a symptom, they promise a way to sidestep conflicts about intimacy; as a dream, they express a wish for relationships with limits, a way to be both together and alone." Turkle's discussion of online companionship suggests there is an anxiety about intimacy experienced currently that might be drawing people to the potentials of technology, offering "ways to be in relationships and protect ourselves from them at the same time" (2011, xii). She looks at the question of intimacy in relation to our "devices." "Digital connections and the social robot may offer the illusion of companionship without the demands of friendship. Our networked life allows us to hide from each other, even as we are tethered to each other."

But these factors pulling people in are not perhaps based on appraisal of what is on offer from technology. "We don't seem to care what these artificial intelligences 'know' or 'understand' of the human moments we might 'share' with them. At the robotic moment, the performance of connection seems connection enough."

And she explains this in terms of "Darwinian buttons," evolutionary traits that might cause us to confuse the robotic response with the one we seek. The construction of sociable robots—both physical care bots and algorithms—make use of our anthropomorphism, "how we see robots as close to human if they do such things as make eye contact, track our motion, and gesture in a show of friendship." Because we are psychologically prone not only to nurture what we love but to love what we nurture, then even "simple artificial creatures" can provoke heartfelt attachment.

While people in Turkle's survey compare pets with therapeutic robots that keep them company, the comparison is not "on all fours." The dog and cat (and other mammals) have a sympathetic nervous system like ours, that links the animal's survival to a system of emotional responses that steer it holistically through its environment. This was an important element of Darwin's observation of evolution about which he wrote in *The Expression of the Emotions in Man and Animals*.

It is not just that the dog, like the child, learns by accumulating myriad layers of call-and-response—this much they may have in common with a self-learning robot. But it is that this call-and-response works as a bloc of feelings that coheres in a felt reality. It marks the affinity that pets offer. While our dogs may not understand why we are sad, they clearly can recognize the affect because they have their own version of it. (This is Turkle's "shared experience"). More to the point, in having this, the dog detects emotion in us as the way in which she has entered into sociality with her own pack since well before she was our "best friend." The dog can be a friend precisely because she uses the communion of an emotional milieu as we do.

In a way, we are better able to conceive of the lack of synchrony in a robot when we think of how other people can disappoint us. If I reach out to a friend, but she is too busy to respond, then I may feel disappointed—almost literally, refused the appointment with a milieu of feeling that I customarily have when we "meet." The way this pleasurable process of friendship can fail, or can be interrupted, shows us what is at stake in the virtue of authenticity.

And in the inauthentic interaction—when, say, the call-center voice starts out friendly because it wants to solicit a donation—we have our clue to the shortcomings of simulation. It is not only that we want to be greeted with friendship "for ourselves" and not for the instrumental purpose that we can supply. We want to have that milieu proposed to us by the other person as an end in itself. That the intersubjective is a milieu of pleasure is at the nub of why other creatures who don't "do" life as feeling cannot produce that synchrony for us. And that even the most difficult, selfish and resistant human beings present us with the reality that there is such a milieu where human meeting happens (in their very act of withholding it).

This is why it seems likely that robot-human communion is something like a category error (trying to get "blood from a stone"). But the simulation of comfort is fascinating from the other direction, for what it draws from the psychotic mental state. Hearing voices, seeing visions, imagining threats—these distressing disturbances of real perception are a product of the psychical capacity called "projection" which is the conduit of our cognitive as well as our emotional lives. To the extent artificial intelligence (and more generally the commodity) gratifies our need instrumentally, it does so through a one-way mirror that we ourselves hold up.

## other models of other minds

IN TRYING TO bring into focus whether the online program for depression is really meeting a need or merely manipulating it, we need to explore how it is that talking to a therapist might be curative. The therapist is no doubt doing more than listening sympathetically. But even this skill, of listening, is a curious exchange not easily simulated.

Turing's was a test of "passing"; can the deceit be detected while talking through the door? Text, of course, was the medium for the deception; the seeming and the plausible replaced the genuine, as it does with the sex bots online.

But what did Turing think we were doing, listening at doors and on the other side of walls? What kind of model of human interaction was he imagining? In other theoretical worlds—those of phenomenology and psychoanalysis—the possibility of knowing each other relies on embodied cues in an affective milieu.

The Turing test is an elegant test of artificial intelligence. But it is not how our interactions with each other really work. In fact, we exert a gravitational pull on each other in a way that defies the instrumental model of other minds. My witnessing of you prompts psychical change in both of us, and it is the synchrony itself that satisfies. This is the abiding satisfaction of love.

This is captured more nearly in the postulations of "psychoanalytic transference." The concept of transference met with in therapy is proposed by Freud as a species of love, but as I discuss elsewhere (in chapter 5 of *Passion in Theory*), as an artificial kind, induced in the analytic setting for the purpose of producing the cure. Transference is necessarily one-sided, because it is through the analyst allowing the attachment of the patient to take place as an immediate experience of love that old unconscious patterns of attachment to the love object can be revealed. It is important to the treatment that the therapist not respond or reciprocate to the emotion expressed, but instead interpret it for the patient for what it says about his or her dispositions, particularly those that are causing present mental pain.

Expressed as a concept in psychoanalytic treatment, the transference can sound recondite and even fanciful. Yet it provides a gauge of the mechanism by which we engage with others in ordinary life, and why some people become our intimates. The assumptions about how to love are learned from earliest infancy, according to Freudian theory, and yet are revived with the vivacity of present experience in each new attachment we form to an object of love.

Behind this notion is a very different model of other minds than that assumed by Turing's imitation game. While the therapist, too, is interpreting an inner world from the evidence of the outer—the speech and sometimes the silence of the therapeutic session—the observations are coming from the projecting into their shared milieu of historical patterns and expectations. In this, psychoanalysis shares a phenomenological view of other people that does not instrumentalize them. This view is articulated, for example, by Maurice Merleau-Ponty.

Synchrony is more than sharing. It is a bodily resonance. In "The Intertwining—The Chiasm" in *The Visible and The Invisible*, Merleau-Ponty puts it into the intersubjective milieu that precedes and underpins our consciousness and self-consciousness. If this milieu is the place of our "meeting of minds," of our sympathy and of our intimacy, then simulation is not the same event, even if it mimics one half of it—our response to learned cues in voice and body. As he writes in *Phenomenology of Perception*: "Truth does not inhabit only the inner man, or more accurately, there is no inner man; man is in the world, and only in the world does he know himself."

## what is a mood?

THE EMOTIONAL PAIN of the one Merleau-Ponty writes of, struggling with intimacy and calling for love's relief, is a demand to find oneself in that world where one can know oneself by being known. We recognize the pain as that of depression.

In modern psychiatry, depression is called a mood disorder. The mood is a founding concept of psychobiology as described in the classification of "mood disorders" in the *Diagnostic and Statistical Manual of Mental Disorders*, aka the DSM. Psychiatry has a checkered history, of discovering malaises at just the point when it can offer a treatment for them. The history of the DSM shows a growing edge of psychological disorders taking shape around the drug therapies designed to treat them. Antidepressants are emblematic technologies in this regard.

Antidepressants are the commonly prescribed remedy for, as the pharmacological manipulation of, affect and mood. In *The Antidepressant Era*, David Healy notes that in many respects "the discovery of antidepressants has been the invention of and marketing of depression" (1997, 5). He describes antidepressant pharmacology, and the rise of a biological language that it gave rise to, as processes that included the need of the pharmaceutical industry to sell product.

The first antidepressants were discovered by accident by a Swiss company while treating tuberculosis patients after World War II. In the 1980s, new forms of antidepressant like Prozac came onto the scene and became so widely prescribed as to gain notoriety in popular culture. Prozac's success showed the huge global market for antidepressants, but also implicated the close ties between drug development and changes in psychiatric diagnosis. Fears of a new "cosmetic psychopharmacology" that came with the impact of Prozac, in which "reshaping your personality would be as easy has highlighting your hair" (as Peter Kramer put it in *Listening to Prozac*) were not realized. But the converse appeared to take place—the malaise of depression became more and more widespread.

Today, cases of depression have ballooned almost 20% in a decade, WHO reports, making it "the leading cause of disability worldwide." The number of people globally living with depression, according to a revised definition, had reached 322 million in 2015, up 18.4% since 2005.

The treatment for depression, if it is not medicated with antidepressants, is currently cognitive behavior therapy. CBT is a regime like pharmacy but without drugs. It mimics pharmacological action by taking an approach to mood that minimizes it as a kind of thought, instead imagining it more on the model of artificial intelligence in need of "reprogramming."

In this, CBT could be said to suppress depression, rather than cure it, much in the manner that a painkiller masks pain but does not necessarily remove the nerves at its source. And viewed as a textual strategy, we could describe CBT as a "third person" discourse that disavows its own status as thought. That it thinks, or that its own thinking has anything to do with the depressive's thought of self-destruction, is suppressed in a clinical-scientific pose which is actually a way of washing one's hands of thinking.

Arguably, because of this, CBT might aggravate depression since despair and hopelessness intensify in the face of the clinician/program that insists: "I know nothing of your pain—your pain is not reasonable. Cheer up, observe how others do it. Fake it until you make it." CBT texts usurp the place of the "second person" of psychotherapy, which treats thought with fellow-feeling, as from one thinker to another. CBT offers little guarantee of relief, since its instrumental mode does not meet the demand that depressive thinking puts to the world: "Why go on living when living is so painful?"

"What is the psychical point of a mood?" asks psychoanalyst Julia Kristeva. She argues depression is key to understanding it. "A life that is unliveable, heavy with daily sorrows, tears held back or shed, total despair, scorching at times, then wan and empty," she writes in *Black Sun*. She draws an eloquent portrait of depression and the person it afflicts. When you are struck down by its black mood, you experience it somatically and at the same time as an idea—a "psychomotor retardation" that slows life to a crawl.

Historically, depression has not always been pathologized, Kristeva writes. Some philosophical sources, such as Aristotle, considered it a naturally occurring variant on the human temper. Kristeva identifies the potential for the work of creativity through art and intellectual life to relieve depression. Kristeva talks of writing in particular as a counter-depressant and points to the therapeutic role that creativity plays in mental self-protective strategies, illustrated in the biographies of countless writers.

Although potentially lethal, depression is graphically expressive of human psychical architecture, in Kristeva's view. It depicts a disturbance of the relation between the self and its (love) object that, adapting Melanie Klein, she regards as central to subjectivity.

## to talk or take a pill

THE ANGUISH OF depression and the travesties of its treatment mark the edge of the implausibility of instrumental rationality, both as an account of the world and of ourselves. A discursive gulf between body, brain, mind, and soul has opened up in postmodernity as a consequence of its divided ontologies.

"To talk or take a pill?," Kristeva asks. Two routes to the same end of relief, they nevertheless make no sense of each other. Is depression best treated with psychotherapy or with drugs? Which is also a way of asking, is feeling a physical or a mental thing?

But the difference between mind and brain remains opaque, and the mood lies along its fault line. Neuroscience can give us quite precise information about the brain's functioning from a chemical point of view—and psychotropic drugs are proof of this. And yet they can tell us precisely nothing about the contents of our visions. Despite rapid advances in pharmacology, the dilemma has only intensified. How do we get from one discourse to the other? How do we re-image our sense of self—and from the clinical side, our view of the subject—when something as intimate as how we feel, especially about being in the world at all, can be interrupted chemically without nevertheless providing insight?

Philosophers of mind tend to ascribe the affective to an "epiphenomenon" that runs over the surface of electrochemical currents in the brain, giving off thought as a kind of luminescence. But in psychoanalysis, it is crucial to drive theory that the affect belongs to the mind and the body, as a signal crossing this threshold and active in both realms. It is this liminal status that makes the question, "to talk or take a pill?," so potent. We can imagine intervening from either direction and via either discourse, the chemical and the psychological, to more or less therapeutic effect.

It is hard to deny the efficacy of modern drugs to treat bodily pain. But in a more metaphysical sense, could we expect pain relief from Big Pharma? We now have the commodification of feeling. To talk versus to take a pill are almost consumer choices as encountered today; at best, a choice between therapeutic alternatives presented as ontological equivalents. But between "to talk" and "to take a pill" lie vastly different philosophical territories, alienated by the plight of the "split subject" in modernity.

As Sarah Beardsworth summarizes it, a piece of reality has "come to grief." That piece is the experience of value. It may be that our ideas (including of ourselves) in "the talk" have become severed analytically from our bodies that are medicated by the taking of a pill. The feelings, the mood, the affect, remain strung between them in a distressing attenuation that, on the instrumental model, has no explanation.

As the experience of emotional pain becomes life threatening, its explanation becomes ontologically urgent. Beyond the instrumental, there needs to be a philosophy of the creation of value, of the space between the talk and the pill.

BETWEEN PSYCHOLOGY AND sociology we dwell as hapless "desiring subjects." Now we are morphing, under the pressures of the technological and the digital, to remake our most personal adventures in intimacy mean something new.

It is in private domains, in the intimate arrangements of love and self-love, that the frauds of freedom are most keenly felt. From dating agencies to internet porn, the connection between self and other threatens to become thoroughly transactional. We need to go via Turing's black box to understand what it is that we want from others, when we desire and when we say we care.

The red herrings of the chat bot and the sex robot disguise the incurable pain of living in an instrumental world. What can be done to remedy it, when bodily need is separated off from psychical satisfaction and treated as something commodified? We try to find love on the internet. Or the dissatisfaction is medicalized—taking the latest antidepressant promoted by Big Pharma.

There is currently a world depression pandemic, as declared by WHO. Julia Kristeva analyses depression as a disturbance of the relation between self and love object. Her critique calls up a question with ontological significance—"To Talk or Take a Pill?"

# *[eight]*

# *[free thought]*

## new logic

FREE ASSOCIATION ISN'T random, it is just unrestrained by ordinary logical processes. The point is not so much what the display in the window sells, but what it markets generically. It teaches the consumer how to think.

The dollar sign attached to each individual object serves to link them in a series of equivalent commodities. Buy this—or this—or this. Good—Better—Best. On whatever basis the series is constructed—price, features, new release or brand name—it is grounded in similarity. The series connects terms, not through narrative, historical, causal or logical consequences, but through likeness (and predominantly visual likeness) that can be played on forward or rewind.

What creates value in these objects is their similarity. The sequence protects, supports, and promotes their differences into an intelligible whole. The concern is not with causes but with effects; it emphasizes surface over depth. Association is propelled by sameness into streams of images in consumer culture. What cannot be visualized in the overwhelming deluge, the really different, becomes radically invisible. It disappears from the catalog of the real.

OPERATING SYSTEMS ON most viewing devices include an inbuilt function for taking a screenshot.

The screenshot is an image, and it creates an image of the screen at a particular time—a freeze frame in the flow of screen images. The screenshot can record a webpage when you can't download it, which gives it a function as information. But it has now become more than this. The screenshot can frame specifics while capturing their social and commercial context in the menu bars and pointers. It can register the currency and poignancy of the subject in pictures, precisely because it is a record of the screen as an event at a specific time.

The screenshot epitomizes the free associative thinking that seems to follow from the internet. For example, it has become a device for self-consciousness and socializing around the technological image. The idea of the screenshot is increasingly used by social media users to record what appears on screen (typically on a smart phone) to share with other users.

Tech savvy cohorts also use the screenshot to underline the technology itself—for example, "error" codes that amuse are circulated as screenshots, or "first aid" photo-editing is done using the zoom function. We take up into our image stream the signs of the meaningful moment—these become what social media users refer to as the "meme."

Wikipedia sources the meme as a unit of meaning to Richard Dawkins' discussion of genes in the 1970s. But the meme began its public life much earlier in the twentieth century in the philosophy of the American pragmatist philosopher Charles Peirce. Looking at the meme through his work produces a different genealogy. Peirce was one of the first to go beyond ordinary language to analyze the meaning of other systems of signs, an area of study that became known as semiology.

Peirce, Barthes, and other semiologists and semioticians showed that anything could become a sign. Not just letters and numbers, but things in the real world and cultural artifacts could become part of a system of meaning, wherever the image of it came to represent a meaning. And more dynamically, semiologists identified that a sign took its meaning in its unique contrast with other and different signs, to which it was related. These contrasts were specific to the sign system in which they were embedded: there was no such thing as a single sign. Everything meaningful took on its meaning in the contrast with other units of meaning within the system.

In internet culture, the "meme" continues to pick out the unit of social meaningfulness, uniquely expressive in a sea of media images that can form from screen gestures and photos to cartoons, video segments, and broadcasts. They are images before they are memes; they need to become images to become memes. This is the seed that sows the virtual, the condition of the possibility of a virtual world—of which the internet is just one actualization.

Important to this process is the fact that the screenshot is free. Anyone who can display the internet image can take a screenshot of it regardless of the status of the material displayed. The screenshot is also free in the sense of being freely available and therefore not rare, confined to a context, or bound up in practical complications. For this reason, the screenshot has no monetary value in and of itself. It's an almost-trivial manifestation of the image it reproduces, showing how theoretically infinite is the reproducibility of the digital image.

The screenshot is emblematic of the cluster of questions presented to thinking by the internet. The internet, as the materialization of free association and the systemic deployment of an image logic, is key to a "teletechnological" (the word is Derrida's) model of creating value. It is through the action of the image that its associations are transmissible, and that investments compound and proliferate. Things rendered as images become thinkable as objects of exchange. Memes become bound to a form of cultural transmission that theorists have labeled viral, and which some have gone as far as to describe in terms of an evolutionary metaphor, claiming they evolve via a kind of "fitness test."

This making of memes is exemplary of value creation in the era of the internet. The internet is changing culture, and not just by changing how it is displayed and disseminated. The web is changing how culture becomes legible. In doing so, cultural values are being transformed. A new logic is being installed. In this free thought, the tropes of freedom and even of democracy are changed. The way cultural products are created and disseminated is dramatically conditioned by the internet and demonstrates a shift in underlying modes of expression and intelligibility. These new modes carry their own philosophical tendency, ones quite unlike the traditional enlightenment logic that has driven cultural values in the nineteenth and twentieth centuries. The virtual intensifies the logic of the image.

And the internet itself is morphing. If it wasn't always hopelessly naïve, the internet as an image of freedom—a free community of information freely given—is now corrupted by its capture in the nets of commerce. The action of the internet as a kind of virtuality has meant making the world into the image of the commodity. It means that the internet and the digital disruption it initiates are practical illustrations of the remaking of values. The logic of the image is undoing value systems and reassembling them on different principles of association, and along different lines.

## the action of the image

HOW CAN IMAGES create values?

"Unsee this!" dares the billboard, proving the point of its own impact. Of course you can't. Images act on us before we are aware of them; they enter our nervous systems, before our cognitive faculties, as objects of sensation. And, by this simple route, they elicit responses that are like our responses to other things—immediately experienced as perceptions. Because of this, images engender belief. They also provoke feelings about what they depict, which is the nervous system preparing to take action.

We now absorb the visual image as an everyday occurrence so that the distinction between the perception and the hallucination—previously a hallmark of psychosis—becomes more complicated. What is real life when we live with the realities of war-torn African nations, natural catastrophes on the Indian subcontinent, or financial crises on Wall Street in the everyday of our lounge rooms?

What I am calling the "action of the image" is just this equivalence, to the nervous system, of the image or any other sight experienced as an object of sensation. The primary operation of "seeing is believing" means the image is a privileged kind of representation. Although we feel we know the difference between images and the real thing, nevertheless there is a residue in our encounter with the image that engenders belief. More, the image solicits our connection with it; we have already taken it in, been taken in by it, from when it enters the eye unbidden, and long before judgment has made its mark on it.

The psychology of object-relations observes our connection with the world through our objects that exist for us by becoming in some sense part of us. But the object can only be taken into ourselves by proxy as an image. The first step in building our relations with the world is to bring into our psychic space the images of things external, but meaningful, to us.

"[O]bject-relations are at the center of emotional life," as Melanie Klein wrote in *Envy and Gratitude*. Object-relations theory postulates that our psychical stability is created and maintained from infancy to adulthood through the mediating work of our internalized objects. Some, our "love objects," become especially formative in that. The relation to the image is a privileged one that arises bodily and is potent psychically.

The contemporary world is alive with images in a way that literally wasn't dreamed of a century ago. Our everyday experience is now populated with images offering sensations that are tendentious. They solicit desire, and create candidates for real things in our lives.

From the beginnings of photography in the late nineteenth century, we were presented with a sensory anomaly; an image that represents a scene that was not present to us in reality. Belief was not difficult; in fact, it was hard to resist. Through the development of cinema and video, to the explosion of images that populate the internet, images now enter our consciousness and condition our milieu in ways that were unthought of in the days when only the artist could create an "uncanny likeness" to real life.

As consumers, we develop a sophistication in reading images without ever needing to become aestheticians. And yet, the nervous system continues its primal meeting with images as objects of sensation, as if they were equivalent at some level with every other sense perception we receive.

This explosion of images has coincided with the rise in dominance of the commodity. In the efflorescence of image and commodity, a new kind of logic has been born. The commodity and the image converge in a vital way. The commodity is much more than a thing—it is a thing that has become an image. Perceived as a want, and in such a way that I can imagine having it, the action of the image as a subjective operation precedes and supports the logic of the commodity.

Both the image and the commodity are pre-packaged to enter into the self-object relation, offering a form of attachment that is easily ingested. The image and the commodity (which is a form of it) do not resist attachment; they solicit it. It is largely the point of the commodity to offer itself as the object of desire.

Julia Kristeva fears that the laminating of the media image with the mental in the flood of imaging now made available on screen is leaving the psychological subject "stranded in the imaginary." The pain of this is commonly separated from its psychical toxicity only by pharmacology. This is the nightmarish world Kristeva depicts at the opening of *New Maladies of the Soul*: (post)modern life having disabled the psychic as an apparatus in the subject, now offers an artificial soul as a prosthetic for the "amputation of subjectivity."

In her function as a clinical psychoanalyst, she writes of the confusion of the psychic imaginary with the photographic flows of media images. Through this flow, Kristeva portrays the emotional dissatisfaction experienced in a world of simulacra. She describes a world in which psychical processes are continuously foreclosed by the double action of a pharmacological and image stream.

On Kristeva's diagnosis, the body now conquers the invisible territory formerly known as the soul. "You are overwhelmed with images, they carry you away, they replace you, you are dreaming," she writes. The body, or at least a particular secular version of it depicted in neuroscience and biology, has called into question the function of the mind. "If drugs do not take over your life, your wounds are 'healed' with images, and before you can speak about your states of the soul, you drown them in the world of mass media" (1989, 8).

The psychical space of ideas and feelings are primarily of image-objects which become the mental devices by which we can attach things to our understanding. Kristeva builds out of this model of the virtual an idea of a layer of images in the psyche, and a virtual pool of imaginings from which we devise our more structured thoughts and expectations and to which are attached hopes and fears.

These become bound into complexes of meaning through which the world can be experienced as satisfying. This process is critical for mental health and explains why the image is a privileged object. Images function psychically as the receptacle of feelings. The image holds the affect for us in a way quite unlike more cerebral ideas and thoughts, as shown in literature, music, and art.

Despite being a "synthetic" kind of experience, image flows occurring outside the individual get taken up and fused in the mind with psychic image flows of the actual and the real—"the psychic life of modern individuals wavers between somatic symptoms (getting sick and going to the hospital) and the visual depiction of their desires (daydreaming in front of the TV). In such a situation, psychic life is blocked, inhibited and destroyed" (1989, 9).

The discursive chasm continues to perplex us, while we create a living model of it in the internet and live streaming that transforms our world. Approaching the mental image on the model of television could permit us to observe that the physical transmission of the vision, in pulses of electricity that align points of light according to a pre-arranged code of pixels, is undeniably its material support, yet the meaning of what is shown arises in a radically different space. The screen is an array of light but the worlds that unfold out of it are legion, significant and not describable through electrochemistry.

In French sociologist Jean Baudrillard's writing on the "hyperreal" and the impact of the image as a substitute for reality is piquantly examined. In *Simulacra and Simulations*. Baudrillard develops a schema of relations between the image and its referent, the simulation and the simulacra that casts it as an event of devolving religiosity.

The congruence of a sign and its reality was guaranteed in the icon, which substituted for the divine only to strengthen its reality as a presence behind the sign, he analyses. But as the faith that the divine lay behind it has ebbed away, the image has detached, moving from its status as a copy of the real original and a substitute, toward being seen as a simulation of it or a model for it. And from there, increasingly the image is an evocation of an absence of referential anchoring that Baudrillard captures in the concept of "simulacrum."

> Abstraction today is no longer that of the map, the double, the mirror or the concept. Simulation is no longer that of a territory, a referential being or a substance. *It is the generation by models of a real without origin or reality:* a hyperreal. (1994, 179, my emphasis)

The image no longer gestures toward its reality; instead it creates its own reality-stream, as in the televising of the Gulf War which Baudrillard saw as no longer a record of a terrestrial conflict but instead as a spectacle conceived for tele-viewing. No casualities, no territories or fighters lost, no blood: merely tracer fire flying across the night sky over an archetypal metropolis.

The moral consequence of this simulation is barbed: no longer can the old verities of the image standing for a reality protect us from harm. The image has become psychically unbound, externalized in terrifying simulacra of worlds.

## devices and desires

THE SMART PHONE has become like a valet, arranging your life in terms that make it livable. The smart phone is an object that does your thinking for you.

You use its calculator to do what you used to do as mental arithmetic. You use its camera as a repository, and perhaps a substitute, for memory. The calendar is your social secretary, nudging you to your "two o'clock." You keep track of time with it. You keep track of money with it. In fact, you even use it as money with a cashless payment app.

You use it to find out where you are, and to navigate, with the map app. When waiting anywhere, it is an indispensable amusement, with its podcasts and news apps. It's the library in your pocket, the encyclopedia, research assistant and broker of disputes at the dinner table. "Who was that guy in . . .?"

You can even talk to it, and "Siri" will answer you and perform things for you. It makes you feel powerful, with a surge of attachment for this shiny and incredibly useful object.

And yet. Are you really sure who is master and who slave? Now you can't add up to save your life, you're lost without the calendar to tell you where to be when, you no longer remember the phone numbers of your friends and relations (or even your own). You need the phone to move funds or record your steps or summon an Uber. And that's before you even make a call on this (uncannily) smart phone.

This was your instrument but now you are beholden to it and dependent on it. And meanwhile, it is reporting on you behind your back. Like a jealous lover, it has you under surveillance wherever in the wide world you are roaming, discoverable by mobile phone towers and revealed by your purchases and searches. Or perhaps more like a handler, relaying your information faithfully to the powers that be, the marketers and advertisers who pay well for it.

This is surely what Martin Heidegger, in his essay "The Question Concerning Technology," had in mind (despite not imagining, much less owning, a smart phone) when he described technology's mode of engaging the world as one of challenging it. While the windmill turns at the mercy of the wind, the power station—even the wind-powered one, and even more so the coal-fired—"puts to nature the unreasonable demand that it supply energy that can be extracted and stored as such" (1983, 320).

And: "a tract of land is challenged into the putting out of coal and ore. The earth now reveals itself as a coal mining district, the soil as a mineral deposit." It no longer appears in its own aspect as anything in itself. All is translated into the idea of a "standing-reserve" for the instrumental purposes of the technologist. The danger as he foresaw was that the technological would eventually deliver up even the human as a standing-reserve, and indeed with population control and mass marketing this has come to pass. Worse: "The threat to man does not come in the first instance from the potentially lethal machines and apparatus of technology. The actual threat has already affected man in his essence" (1983, 333).

In this sense, Heidegger saw the danger of technology was a spiritual one, not only infecting others who become a standing-reserve but a habit of thought in which even the self becomes trapped. It's hard to avoid the suspicion that this dystopia has arrived, in the form of the internetted world bound in all its fibers to the instrumental-mercantile.

Heidegger's argument is that technology is first and foremost a way of thinking. It is a style of thought that works by challenging the representation to fit a particular form. It has a proliferant habit; the idea of the rational—as used for example in the term "economic rationalism"—presumes to take over the whole of thinking, even the name of thinking, for instrumental means/ends. In the light (or maybe it is in the shadow) of instrumental thinking, no other thinking makes sense anymore.

## automated thought

CONSUMER LOGIC IS built on an array of elementary contrasts that also power the logic of the binary in general. The importance of this conceptual isomorphism cannot be overestimated. As code, it generates the digital. The simple on/off distinction, reiterated many millions of times, produces whole networks of distinction that can describe the workings of devices, no less than of data. And arranged in layers of contrasts, the binary logic builds the intelligibility of an image stream.

The binary opposition is a prefabricated idea, a shorthand for thinking that forestalls thinking. Ironically, at the same time as it was being diagnosed in the work of structuralism as the prime mechanism of signification, it was being put to work as technology to produce the digital. It became an extreme application of an instrumentalism that already was taking shape as the *force majeure* of the age.

An associative logic drives instrumentalism in another register with the same fluency and ease of object-relations, as means to ends. Seeing something as its objective function for a subject, in its fitness for purpose for a desiring self, conceives of the world according to a binary judgment (self vs. other) that blinds us to its other aspects—those ways in which this thing is not an object, and not intelligible as an object of consumption.

Conceptually, it is that very operation of the oscillation between on and off that is the instrument. It is a kind of value and a type of judgment right there in the switch. On or Off. The harnessing of that, in devices as large as the online market or as small as the iPhone and in representations as elaborate and yet ephemeral as the internet webpage, gives us the galloping instrumentalism of the global technological world.

"The origin of technology is nothing technological." The conceptual origin of technology is the means/ends logic, but it is also the conceptual binary of the on and the off.

Judgments proliferate in a digitized world that uses layers of these switches—on/off, up/down, black/white, good/bad, right/wrong—spawned into whole networks of values in which we are required to live. Swipe right/left. It happens with discourse as much as with material code.

The automated thinking of binaries culminates in algorithms that risk taking thought—its burden and its opportunity—from us. The physicist Stephen Hawking, despite being dependent on machines to keep him alive, nevertheless warned against the rise of artificial intelligence in a BBC interview in 2014.

Artificial intelligence emerges from the binary code as a kind of automation of judgment, a thousand thousand tiny choices made by the program, programmed into the algorithm. And actually, in the exponential automation of self-learning artificial intelligence, it is as if a thousand thousand tiny tendencies to judge have been pre-programmed.

Take as an example, the automation of the stock market. The automation of the production of economic value through the tireless operation of algorithms enabled globalized production and a system of world trade that made whole populations wealthy. It also produced a disaster as large as the Global Financial Crisis. That the judgment (to buy, to sell) was automated was part of the perfect storm; the digitizing of the financial world and indeed of the whole economic habitat, had come about through weaponizing the binary code in algorithms. The algorithm is the network of completely digital forms, automated value judgments that turn themselves on and off—and which, at scale, escalated the catastrophe.

The algorithm is the converse of "free" thought. But binary is critiqued in Derrida's theory of deconstruction; a kind of rhetorical device, the opposition drives thought like a kind of machine for making meaning and establishing value.

## form guide

WHEN I WANT something online, I am often asked to register. The screen throws up a form I'm required to fill out with name, address, email, password. The online form is used to sign consumers up to everything from shopping to credit, from health care to tax.

Every transaction on the net invites me to open an account, disclosing my identity and personal details in order to part with money. When I supply this information, the merchant has captured "for marketing purposes" details that, paired with the interest I have displayed in their particular merchandise, is a valuable commodity of itself.

This information can be on-sold for other marketing lists even if I don't buy anything from the site. So I have given them something for free, even though it was I who was the customer. In almost every transaction in the virtual world through my meta-data I give something other than what I receive, and I often give it unwittingly.

The online form massages me into the expectation behind the transaction. Providing suitable contact details, bank details and so on all require the consumer to be located in the world in such a way as to supply these. It doesn't work, for example, for me to be "of no fixed address"; it isn't easy to pay with cash. It often also requires further "authorization"; the credit card, the driver's license, the social security number, the passport and other indicators of social membership.

We often express our exasperation with the "administrivia" that encroaches in everyday life, regarding it as an annoying impost. The form-filling for everything, from buying a dog to getting a divorce, we think of as mere paperwork and red tape getting in our way. But this view may be too sanguine about the power of the bureaucratic to institute its own forms of life. How things are classified tells us how we are to regard them. The form things take will take on a naturalness and a self-evidence as a result of the order imposed by classification. But more, it intimates how things will regard us if we submit (to) the form.

The form nominates categories in which to live—"business traveler" (frequent flyer membership, and Fringe Benefits Tax liability), "single mother" (social security and the welfare system), "home owner" (mortgage finance, local council rates). Then it pushes you into them. The form nominates a date not of your choosing by which you must comply and then proceeds to punish you if you miss the timetable. In this way, it insinuates its authority.

Underpinning the idea of bureaucracy is the power of ordering. Michel Foucault wrote in *The Order of Things* of "all the ordered surfaces and all the planes with which we are accustomed to tame the wild profusion of existing things." He was quoting from a fictitious Chinese encyclopedia classification of animals, which the writer Borges had devised as a way of demonstrating the cultural specificity of any ordering:

> Animals are divided into: (a) belonging to the Emperor, (b) embalmed, (c) tame, (d) sucking pigs, (e) sirens, (f) fabulous, (g) stray dogs, (h) included in the present classification, (i) frenzied, (j) innumerable, (k) drawn with a very fine camelhair brush, (l) et cetera, (m) having just broken the water pitcher, (n) that from a long way off look like flies.

As Foucault concludes, underlining "the exotic charm of another system of thought, is the limitation of our own, the stark impossibility of thinking that" (1973, xv).

It may be no accident that Borges selects Chinese thought as the figure for "foreign thinking." Administration began with the invention of writing in many parts of the ancient world, but the Chinese system of meritocracy set up in the Han Dynasty, of a bureaucracy staffed by non-elected officials who won their place by competitive exam, was perhaps the longest lived. It ended only in 1905.

Bureaucracy arises historically as a method for control of economic means through taxation. Writing is a preliminary to the document, which has been a primary instrument of bureaucracy from Ancient Egypt on and as early as the beginning of writing the power of the sign and the power of the sovereign were linked. Making a list of particulars, detailing inventories, and writing things down begins the long story of owning them and extracting wealth from them.

The Chinese devised a technology of the seal. The seal placed on a document became the means by which it sprung into the life of power. Vitrines in a room of the Shanghai Museum document the history of seals which were used in China to validate the documents of high-ranking officials as early as 1600 BC. Seals became symbols of power and status and identified the user and his rank. During the Ming Dynasty, seals were common place, stamping documents, official dispatches, and certificates of the inspection of commodities.

The seal was a marker of bureaucratic power because it was both authentic and reproducible. It was possible to make endless marks on innumerable documents multiplying the operation of power while at the same time restricting it completely to the one authorized channel. The seal functioned as more than a signature because, as an object, it had a life of its own. Indeed, the passing of political and dynastic power became embedded in the seal—each new Emperor had to physically possess the seals before he could exercise power. The seal's function was also thereby more than symbolic; stamping a document with it animated the will of the authority—and without its mark incorporated as a material property of it, the document had no force.

When the term "bureaucracy" came into use in European thinking in the eighteenth century it became almost immediately pejorative. It was the sociologist Max Weber who made a systematic analysis of the importance of the bureaucratic to the efficient organization of human affairs. In particular, bureaucratic ordering developed as the vehicle for the governing power to exact taxation—even a simple economy requires it to ensure fairness, consistency, and efficiency across trade and government (and then, Weber remarks, a stable system of taxation is also the precondition for bureaucracy). Taking the Chinese system to heart, the British raised bureaucracy to an art form on which was based the success of their entire Empire.

But Weber would not be the last to note that bureaucracy could become oppressive to those under its authority as the inflexible operation of a rules-based rationality. The Byzantine system was famous for it—we still refer to a complicated administrative procedure as "byzantine." Novelists from Kafka to Orwell brought out its danger to the human spirit in fictional portrayals of "bureaucracy gone mad."

Bureaucracy goes mad because of its similarity to the mechanical—the bureaucratic is the most perfect practical extension of an instrumental rationalism and itself thereby a kind of distributed machine or technology. "The fully developed bureaucratic apparatus compares with other organizations exactly as does the machine with the non-mechanical modes of production," Weber observes in *Economy and Society*:

> Once fully established, bureaucracy is among those social structures which are hardest to destroy. Bureaucracy is the means of transforming social action into rationally organized action. . . . Where administration has been completely bureaucratized, the resulting system of domination is practically indestructible. (1968, 987–989)

As he goes on to outline, once the apparatus exists it becomes indispensable, and through its "impersonal" character, becomes a mechanism that, contrasting with feudal loyalty, is "easily made to work for anybody who knows how to gain control over it." The pretender needs merely to "change the top officials." In this way, the bureaucratic apparatus thwarts true revolution by making the "forceful creation of entirely new formations of authority more and more impossible." From when this formation is secured, the place of a revolution is taken by the *coup d'état* which means in effect that, while changing the dancers, the dance remains the same.

Weber notes that bureaucracy is a requirement for the governing of a mass democracy, and the replacement of "grace and favor" strategies by notables close to the prince with the value of a blind justice; the abstract regularity of the exercise of authority, which is a result of the demand for "equality before the law." But while law is its prerequisite, bureaucracy adds something potent to law; it adds the systematizing of authority that eventually produces a form of domination stronger than collective behavior or social action.

The deceptively simple tools of the bureaucrat are the file and the scribe, which together make a "bureau" or office (writes Weber) distinct from a household. Its tone can be said to be the characteristic exercise of "matter of factness" and "expertise." While it may be hard to understand how simply recording things can become a threat to the human, it is the conceptual property of obliging things to fit the category that begets the remarkable power of the bureaucratic.

## technological thinking

HEIDEGGER WAS LED to the conclusion that technology, in essence, was a species of instrumental thinking. Before there are machines and devices, there must be the idea of making the world to fit our own ends, and finding the means to do it. Instrumental thinking itself becomes a kind of technology. Thinking like that allows us to make things work for us, not just in material terms but in the way we conceive of worlds—the social, the political, the economic.

This instrumental thinking about life is powerful and takes many forms. Instrumental thinking has a long history before the internet and economic rationalism. Its emergence with technology at the inception of the secular state was observed by Weber, among others. Ironically, Weber, who had so aptly observed the instrumental indefeasibility of bureaucracy as "a machine," analyzed individual freedom also as beginning from a kind of rationality closely allied to instrumental:

> [W]e associate the highest measure of an empirical "feeling of freedom" with those actions which we are conscious of performing rationally—i.e. in the absence of physical and psychic "compulsions," vehement "affects," and "accidental" disturbances of the clarity of judgment, in which we pursue a clearly conceived "end" through "means" which are the most adequate according to our empirically grounded knowledge.

Quoting this passage, Donald Levine comments: "Weber thereby reiterated the classical idealist equation of rationality and freedom" (2005, 110). But Levine seeks to correct the inflation of instrumental rationality with the whole of rationality in an analysis that points up at least four different kinds of rationalization detectable in Weber's work. And, he points out, the closely related idea of objectification, which appears to underpin the view of rationalism among his German precursors, can be observed to have a positive modality in, for example, Marx's account of "the creation of commodities as an externalization of creative energies that belonged to their human makers."

So, on closer examination, each of the forms of rationalism tendered by this tradition pivot around a distinction between subject and object that is also taken up in a different register in the psychological view of object-relations theory. It points to a nest of philosophical meanings around "the rational" that testify to an intense ambivalence.

Ending his discussion on the fortunes of these rationalisms in the contemporary world, Levine muses on the enormous psychical energies required of the modern urban subject to dwell in the money economy as an employee and as a consumer. That habitat over-emphasizes the conceptual and instrumental orientations at the expense of the affective parts of experience.

> It takes little talent as a social observer in our day to detect the further expansion of this syndrome thanks to the newer technologies of cell phones, Palm Pilots, and Internet Technologies [to which we may add, thirteen years on, the smart phone and Siri]. What is more at the symbolic cultural level, it reflects the heightened prestige of economist thinking. . . . It was a fundamental insight of Weber, as well as of Simmel, that the calculative habits of mind associated with a market economy and its related technology, and with the point of view of his discipline of economics, became inflated in the modern world. This remains a suggestive point of departure for diagnoses of our time. (2005, 120)

The more disturbing pressures of instrumental rationality might come not from the commodity, nor from technology, but from the culture of conformity attendant on the bureaucratic.

Bureaucracy begins as the attempt to think the detail of a practice rationally, to submit it to the means and ends of a "rational" thought that is indifferent to particular thinkers and actors at particular times. It is an effort to schematize the difference of individual particulars of the case. Bureaucracy, as the acting out of the instrumental, continually enacts its danger; the colonizing of experience by a rationality that understands only its own mode, the production of means for similarly produced ends. It is an intelligence of things that recognizes only its own genius, and for which other ways of thinking remain incomprehensible.

The bureaucratic seeks to schematize life under principle. This argument could lead us to more disturbing observations of the latent violence to be found in imposing law on life in general. From the everyday regulation of practices as diverse as sexuality, public speech, family life, and scholarship to the monstrous imposition of principle that became the policy of mass genocide in Nazi Germany, bureaucracy's rational limit is only finally satisfied in destruction of the unruly particular in the name of principle.

In *Origins of Totalitarianism*, Arendt comments on the Soviet anxiety about the playing of "chess for chess's sake." And elsewhere she observes: "Himmler quite aptly identifies the SS member as the new type of man who under no circumstances would ever do 'a thing for its own sake'." To do something for its own sake is to refuse to bring it under the organizing rubric of productivity, patriotism or political correctness. It is a way of insisting on a plurality in things, and to resist the idea that the world can be reduced to only one idea, that governs it.

# *[afterword]*

THE INTERNET SERVES as a focus for the discussion of free stuff and its paradoxes because it is the real-world instantiation of the power of the sign, and a literal rendition of it.

A thread binds the terms commodity, technology, and democracy in their mode of value-production. The concept of commodity is built on exchange, and relies on a style of value-production that operates through norms. Democracy, too, has a technological iteration of the rationality that orders the world according to the subject/object (means/ends) style of thought. As a political genre, democracy fits technology as a subject/object ordering and it also fits well with the commodity, a product of the same distinction. The technology genre produces an equivalence enabling exchange.

"Language is the supreme spectacular value, because it reveals the nothingness of all things; money is the supreme commodity, because in the last analysis it shows the nullity of all commodities," writes Agamben in *Creation and Anarchy* (2019, 74).

Perhaps, within the circuitry of this exchange, the idea of free stuff approaches what Agamben points up as anarchic: "What is in question here is the problem of the 'anarchic' or unfounded character of language, action, and governance." For Agamben, the de-materializing of credit and money is paralleled by the dematerializing of the sign-as-referent. He quotes Guy Debord, *The Society of the Spectacle*—but he might as easily have cited Baudrillard. This is a well-worn track, a speculation that has been developing for at least fifty years in European philosophy. We now see it accomplished in the digital world, especially in the international finance system, and which explains its strange ontological status. That status twins credit without security, sign without reference; the pure commodification of speculating.

The dire depiction of the theoretical landscape is shared by several theorists following from Nietzsche—Benjamin to Baudrillard, Adorno to Agamben, and even Zizek. It is, we might say, a European malaise. But it had not received the same attention in Anglo-American philosophy, perhaps because the American economic trajectory has profited so thoroughly from capitalism.

Now it almost seems as though the temptation to declare the end of everything has taken hold on both sides of the aisle. This is what Derrida had in his sights in 1984 when he called for "no apocalypse, not now," and which is echoed more recently in the work of Jean-Luc Nancy and others, as "the equivalence of catastrophes." It is through the deconstructive procedures of such writers that the logic that powers the internet, and that derives from the digital, can be critiqued.

The binary is a unit of contrast—on or off—that sets a chain of association in motion. *Like this, only different.* The movement happens most obviously through visuals, and this is why the internet is so at home with this way of representing things.

And yet, this kind of logic is quite specific and rules out other kinds of thinking. This mode of thinking has come to proliferate and dominate as seen in the thinking of the meme, from social media through its origins in semiology. The real effects of commodity, technology and democracy are shaped by effects of representation and these can be described in generic protocols.

States of being that are not expressible within that seriality find their political, social and material being at risk. There may be other ways of thinking and being given in other genres. But we would need to represent them to see them emerge.

AS THIS BOOK is published, a presidential election and Brexit come into effect. But both events are now inundated by the swell of the COVID-19 pandemic across the world. Its automated action demonstrates the power of the viral, as a kind of non-thought and very close to Agamben's category of the anarchic. A misdemeanor in one small point on the globe, linked to the uneasy proximity of the modern and the natural world and amplified by misjudgment, forces the issue upon us all of the material supports of our digital realms.

This sudden devastation is giving the global a wholly unanticipated task for the decade to come, to rebuild and perhaps to refashion that which we value. The fates of freedom and commodity, as twinned in this book, remain opaque.

# *[references]*


Adorno, Theodor. "The essay as form." in *Notes to Literature*. Rolf Tiedemann (ed.). New York: Columbia University Press, 1991.

———. "The culture industry revisited" and "free time." in *The Culture Industry: Selected Essays on Mass Culture*, J. M. Bernstein (ed.). London/New York: Routledge, 1991.

Adorno, Theodor and Horkheimer, Max. *The Dialectic of Enlightenment*, John Cumming (trans). New York: Herder & Herder, 1972.

Agamben, Giogio. *Creation and Anarchy: The Work of Art and the Religion of Capitalism*, Adam Kotsko (trans). Stanford: Stanford University Press, 2019.

Anderson, Chris. *Free: The Future of a Radical Price*. New York: Hyperion Books, 2009.

Arendt, Hannah. *The Origins of Totalitarianism*. New York: Schocken Books, 1951.

———. *The Human Condition*. Chicago: University of Chicago Press, 1958.

———. *Eichmann in Jerusalem: A Report on the Banality of Evil*. New York: Viking Press, 1963.

———. "The image of hell." in *Essays in Understanding 1930–1954*, Jerome Kohn (ed.). New York: Penguin Random House, 2005.

Bakhtin, Mikhail. *Speech Genres and Other Late Essays*. Vern W. McGee (trans) Caryl Emerson & Michael Holquist (eds.). Austen: University of Texas Press, 1986.

Barthes, Roland. *A Lover's Discourse*: *Fragments*, Richard Howard (trans). New York: Hill & Wang, 1979.

———. *Mythologies*, Annette Lavers (trans). New York: The Noonday Press Farrar, Straus & Giroux, 1972.

Baudrillard, Jean. *Simulacra and Simulation*, Sheila Glaser (trans). Ann Arbor: University of Michigan Press, 1994.

———. *The Gulf War Did Not Take Place*, Paul Patton (trans). Bloomington: Indiana University Press, 1995.

Beardsworth, Sara. *Julia Kristeva: Psychoanalysis and Modernity*. State University of New York Press, 2004.

Benjamin, Walter. "Capitalism as religion," (Fragment 74) Chad Kautser (trans). in *The Frankfurt School on Religion: Key writings by the major thinkers*, Eduardo Mendieta (ed.). New York/London: Routledge, 2005.

Bernays, Edward. *Crystallizing Public Opinion*. New York: Boni & Liveright, 1923.

———. *Propaganda*. New York: H. Liveright, 1928.

Bettelheim, Bruno. *The Informed Heart: Autonomy in a Mass Age*. Free Press, 1960.

Butler, Judith. *Precarious Life: The Powers of Mourning and Violence*. Verso, 2004.

Chambers, Nicholas. *Adman: Warhol Before Pop*. Catalogue Art Gallery of NSW, 2017.

Chanter, Tina. *Art, Politics, & Rancière: Broken Perceptions*. London: Bloomsbury, 2017.

Childs, Jason. *The Thought of Literature*. Unpublished doctoral thesis University of Technology Sydney, 2018.

Critchley, Simon. *The Ethics of Deconstruction*. Edinburgh University Press, 1992.

Darwin, Charles. *The Expression of the Emotions in Man and Animals*. John Murray, 1872.

Deleuze, Gilles. *Difference and Repetition*, Paul Patton (trans). Columbia University Press, 1994.

———. *Foucault*, Sean Hand (trans). University of Minnesota Press, 1988.

Derrida, Jacques. *Specters of Marx*, Peggy Kamuf (trans). Routledge, 1993.

———. *Philosophy in a Time of Terror: Dialogue with Jurgen Habermas and Jacques Derrida*. University of Chicago Press, 2003.

———. *Paper Machine*, Rachel Bowlby (trans). Stanford University Press, 2004.

———. *Writing and Difference*, Alan Bass (trans). University of Chicago Press, 1978.

———. "No apocalypse, not now (Full Speed Ahead, Seven Missiles, Seven Missives)" Jacques Derrida; Catherine Porter; Philip Lewis. *Diacritics* 14(2), 1984, 20–31.

Deutscher, Penelope. *Foucault's Futures: A Critique of Reproductive Reason*. Columbia University Press, 2017.

Dillon, Brian. *Essayism: On Form, Feeling and Nonfiction*. Fitzcarraldo Editions, 2017.

Diprose, Rosalyn. *Corporeal Generosity*. New York: SUNY Press, 2002.

Diprose, Rosalyn and Ziarek, Ewa. *Arendt, Natality & Biopolitics*. Edinburgh University Press, 2018.

Engels, Frederick. *The Origin of the Family Private Property & The State*. Chicago: Charles H. Kerr, 1902.

Ferrell, Robyn. *Copula: Sexual Technologies & Reproductive Powers*. SUNY Press, 2006.

———. *Passion in Theory*. London: Routledge, 1996.

Foucault, Michel. *The Order of Things*. Knof Doubleday, 1973.

———. *Discipline and Punish: The Birth of the Prison*. Penguin Books, 1977.

Freud, Sigmund. *The Interpretation of Dreams*, vol. 4, James Strachey (ed.). Standard Edition, 1953.

———. *Papers on Technique,* vol. 12, James Strachey (ed.). Standard Edition, 1953.

Fukayama, Francis. *The End of History and the Last Man*. Free Press, 1992.

Gatens, Moira. *Imaginary Bodies: Ethics, Power, and Corporeality*. Routledge, 1996.

Grace, Helen. "IPO" *Exhibition Catalogue*, John Batten Gallery Hong Kong/Mori Gallery Sydney, 2009.

Healy, David. *The Antidepressant Era*. Harvard University Press, 1997.

Heidegger, Martin. "The question concerning technology." in *Heidegger: Basic Writings*, David Farrell Krell (ed.). Harper Collins, 1983.

Hollander, Anne. *Seeing Through Clothes*. Viking, 1978.

Jones, Paul K. *Critical Theory and Demagogic Populism*. Manchester University Press, 2020.

Kipnis, Laura. *Against Love: A Polemic*. Pantheon, 2003.

Klein, Melanie. *Envy & Gratitude and Other Works, 1946–63* Vol III of the Writings of Melanie Klein Delacourt/Seymour Laurence, New York, 1975.

Kristeva, Julia. *Melanie Klein*. New York: Columbia University Press, 2001.

———. *Black Sun: Depression and Melancholia*, Leon S. Roudiez (trans). Columbia University Press, 1989.

———. *New Maladies of the Soul*, Ross Gubermann (trans). Columbia University Press, 1995.

Latour, Bruno. "Why has critique run out of steam? From matters of fact to matters of concern." *Critical Inquiry* 30(2), 2004, 225–248.

Levine, Donald. "Weber's theory of rational action." in *Max Weber's Economy and Society: A Critical Companion*, C. Camic, P. Gorski & D. Trubek (eds.). Stanford: Stanford University Press, 2005.

Levy, David. *Love and Sex with Robots*. Harper Collins, 2007.

Marx, Karl. *Capital,* vol. 1. Penguin Classics, 2011.

Mauss, Marcel. *The Gift: The Form and Reason for Exchange in Archaic Societies,* W. D. Halls (trans). W.W. Norton, 2000.

Merleau-Ponty, Maurice. *The Visible and the Invisible*, Claude Lefort (ed.). Alphonso Lingis (trans). Evanston: Northwestern University Press, 1968.

Nancy, Jean-Luc. *After Fukushima: The Equivalence of Catastrophes*, Charlotte Mandell (trans). New York: Fordham University Press, 2014.

Nietzsche, Friedrich. *On the Genealogy of Morals* (1887) reproduced in *Basic Writings of Nietzsche*, Peter Gay (intro) Walter Kaufmann (trans). Penguin, 2000.

———. *The Gay Science* (1882) several editions, including W. Kaufmann (trans) Vintage 1974 By Friedrich Nietzsche, Introduction by Peter Gat, Translated by Walter Kaufmann.

Oliver, Kelly. *Reading Kristeva: Unraveling the Double-Bind.* Indiana University Press, 1993.

Piketty, Thomas. *Capital in the Twenty-First Century*, Arthur Goldhammer (trans). Harvard University Press, 2013.

Ricoeur, Paul. *The Rule of Metaphor: Multi-Disciplinary Studies of the Creation of Meaning in Language*, Robert Czerny with Kathleen McLaughlin & John Costello, S. J. (trans). London: Routledge and Kegan Paul, 1978 (1975).

Robertson, Iain. *Understanding Art Markets: Inside the World of Art and Business*. Taylor & Francis, 2015.
Roffe, Jon. *Abstract Market Theory*. Palgrave Macmillan, 2015.
Rose, Gillian. *The Melancholy Science: An Introduction to the Thought of Theodor W. Adorno*. Macmillan, 1978.
Secomb, Linnell. *Philosophy and Love*. Edinburgh University Press, 2007.
Stephens, Elizabeth. "The object of normality." in *Normality: A Critical Genealogy*, Peter Cryle and Elizabeth Stephens (eds.). University of Chicago Press, 2019.
Streek, Wolfgang. "How will capitalism end?" *New Left Review* 87, 2014, 35–64.
Tabbi, Joseph. *Cognitive Fictions*. University of Minnesota Press, 2002.
Turing, Alan. "Computing machinery and intelligence." *Mind* 59(236), 1950, 433–460.
Turkle, Sherry. *Alone Together: Why We Expect More from Technology and Less from Each Other*. Basic Books, 2011.
Warhol, Andy. *The Philosophy of Andy Warhol: From A to B and Back Again*. Harcourt Brace Jovanovich, 1975.
Watson, Don. "Enemy within: American politics in the time of Trump." *Quarterly Essay* 63, 2016.
Weber, Max. *Economy and Society: An Outline of Interpretive Sociology*, 3 vols, Roth, Guenther & Wittich, Claus (eds.). New York: Bedminster Press, 1968.
Wittgenstein, Ludwig. *Lectures and Conversations on Aesthetics, Psychology, and Religious Belief* transcribed from notes by Yorick Smythies, Rush Rhees & James Taylor. University of California Press, 1966.
Zizek, Slavoj. *Living in the End Times*. Verso, 2010.

## ADDITIONAL RESOURCES

### *"free form"*

https://www.smh.com.au/national/judge-in-rush-trial-takes-aim-at-bad-pun-in-king-leer-headline-20181108-p50epd.html
https://mumbrella.com.au/cardinal-pell-verdict-splashed-across-major-australian-newspapers-567388

### *"free gift"*

https://en.wikipedia.org/wiki/Department_store
https://www.bbc.com/news/election-us-2016-36935175

### *"free time"*

mymodernmet.com march 20, 2016 (accessed June 22, 2018)
Hamid Dabashi, Aljazeera 4 Feb 2016 (accessed June 20, 2018)
https://www.labiennale.org/en/art/2015/biennale-arte-2015-all-worlds-futures
https://www.biennaleofsydney.art/archive/20th-biennale-of-sydney/

## "free market"

https://www.pennymacusa.com/blog/understanding-the-roles-of-fannie-mae-and-freddie-mac
https://www.nytimes.com/2016/06/04/arts/design/ai-weiwei-and-warhol-together-again.html
the American Marketing Association: https://www.ama.org/
2002 BBC documentary "The Century of the Self," presenter Adam Curtis.

## "free speech"

https://www.theguardian.com/books/2016/nov/15/post-truth-named-word-of-the-year-by-oxford-dictionaries
https://www.theguardian.com/news/2017/nov/16/a-mission-for-journalism-in-a-time-of-crisis
https://www.theguardian.com/media/2016/jul/12/how-technology-disrupted-the-truth

## "free world"

https://en.wikipedia.org/wiki/Business_model

## "free choice"

http://www.familycourt.gov.au/wps/wcm/connect/fcoaweb/family-law-matters/separation-and-divorce/
http://www.familycourt.gov.au/wps/wcm/connect/fcoaweb/family-law-matters/family-violence/family-violence-best-practice-principles/

## "free love"

https://en.wikipedia.org/wiki/RealDoll
www.thesun.co.uk/tech/2084051/robot-sex-doll-sex-brothel-paris-cost/
https://www.theguardian.com/tv-and-radio/2017/dec/01/sex-robots-are-coming-review-documentary
www.nhs.uk/conditions/stress-anxiety-depression/self-help-therapies/#apps-and-online-tools-for-mental-health
http://content.time.com/time/health/article/0,8599,1952143,00.html
http://broughttolife.sciencemuseum.org.uk/broughttolife/techniques/antidepressants
https://healingfromdepression.com/antidepressant-therapy/
https://www.ncbi.nlm.nih.gov/pmc/articles/PMC4428540/
http://www.who.int/news-room/fact-sheets/detail/depression

## "free thought"

https://theconversation.com/stephen-hawking-warned-about-the-perils-of-artificial-intelligence-yet-ai-gave-him-a-voice-93416

# *[index]*

# *[about the author]*

**Robyn Ferrell** is adjunct professor at the Centre for Law, Art and Humanities at the Australian National University, and in Gender & Cultural Studies at the University of Sydney. She is also a member of the J.M. Coetzee Centre for Creative Practice at the University of Adelaide. Ferrell has published several books of philosophy and cultural studies, including *Sacred Exchanges: Images in Global Context* (2012) and *Copula: Sexual Technologies Reproductive Powers* (2006). She writes regularly on art, writing, and culture for various journals and magazines.

www.ingramcontent.com/pod-product-compliance
Ingram Content Group UK Ltd.
Pitfield, Milton Keynes, MK11 3LW, UK
UKHW041843031026
15587UKWH00002B/976

9 781793 603623